NAT GONELLA

A LIFE IN JAZZ

Ron Brown

with Digby Fairweather

NAT GONELLA

A LIFE IN JAZZ

Published by Northway Publications
39 Tytherton Road, London N19 4PZ, UK.
www.northwaybooks.com
info@northwaybooks.com

Edited by Roger and Ann Cotterrell with Chris Parker.

The publishers acknowledge with thanks the kind permission of copyright holders to reprint the photographs used in this book. Permissions have been sought in all cases where the identity of copyright holders is known.

A CIP record for this book is available from the British Library.

ISBN 0 9537040-7-6

Published 2005

Previous edition published in 1985 as *Georgia on My Mind* by Ron Brown with Cyril Brown.

Printed and bound in Great Britain by Antony Rowe Ltd, Chippenham, Wiltshire.

Contents

Preface

by Humphrey Lyttelton

In countless interviews over the decades, I have been asked how I got into jazz in my youth. I have heard myself intoning like a mantra, over and over again, the name of Nat Gonella. In recent times, the discouraging response has been, 'How do you spell that?' I suppose I shouldn't be surprised. Nat is a legend, and legends depend, for their survival, on constant repetition of the facts and, indeed, the myths too. Whoever it was who said that most memory is fiction had it right. In checking facts for some words to welcome this essential book, I have discovered that much of my memory is a myth.

The fact is that it was Nat Gonella alone whose recordings in the mid-thirties prompted me to cajole (as I was fifteen years old at the time, bully is probably the better word) my mother into buying me a trumpet to supplant the mouth-organ that had been my first medium of jazz expression. It was from Nat Gonella and his Georgians that I learnt tunes such as "Mahogany Hall Stomp', 'Bessie Couldn't Help It', 'I'm Confessin'" and, of course, 'Georgia on My Mind' before Louis Armstrong had fully impinged on my consciousness. I probably owe it to Nat that I have never felt instinctively judgmental about the commercial aspects of Armstrong's repertoire. The first recording of Nat and the Georgians that I possessed had on the A side 'I Can't Dance, I've Got Ants in My Pants'. When I first met him many years later, I confessed to him my lifelong devotion to a tune he sang called 'I'd Like to See Samoa of Samoa'. He guffawed with delight that I should remember such a thing.

It has been for me a pleasure to find, in Digby Fairweather, someone with whom to share memories of Nat. But this book will have a value far beyond the boundaries of nostalgia. It is, after all, about someone who was, in his time, a superstar. In the early thirties, he was signed up eagerly by the leading dance-band leaders – Billy Cotton, Roy Fox, Lew Stone, Ray Noble – in a way suggestive of a present-day football hero. Once at the top, his espousal of the music of Louis Armstrong, both by word and by imitation, transformed a popular music scene that, if it embraced jazz at all, had hitherto been biased towards the white 'New York' school of Bix Beiderbecke and Red Nichols. As for influence, neither Digby nor I have been reticent in our acknowledgements over the years, but it came as a surprise to me to read, in a recent interview given by Bill Colyer, that his brother Ken, high priest of New Orleans purism, had learned to play trumpet from the same Nat Gonella tutor-cum-autobiography that came free with my first trumpet in 1936, and that Ken had based his trumpet-playing posture on photographs of Nat in action. I have no doubt that we three represent just the tip of an iceberg.

At the beginning of this piece, I expressed dismay at the ignorance in much of the present-day media of Nat Gonella's existence and importance. I thank Ron Brown and Digby for giving me something to wave at interviewers in future. But they and I know one person who would not have expected more. When the reissued recording of 'Oh! Mo'nah' by Nat Gonella and his Georgians surprisingly topped the hit parade in Holland, Nat, then seventy years old, was himself interviewed on a special BBC television documentary. He was asked if the success meant that he would be going back on the road. That well-worn face registered his scorn of the idea.

'Nah!' was his response, 'Why would I want to do that? I'm an ol' m-a-an,' (the last word drawn out in true Cockney fashion). Then he added, 'The 'ouse is paid for, the car's paid for, the wife's paid for. . . '

A lovely, unpretentious man.

Humphrey Lyttelton

January 2005

Introduction

Following the publication of *Georgia on My Mind*, my first Nat Gonella biography twenty years ago, more stories arrived from Nat's friends and colleagues. And back in 1985, nobody could know that the subject of this book was destined to add a further thirteen years to his remarkable life! This new volume brings up to date the story of this revered pioneer of British jazz.

For the authors, compiling this biography has been a labour of love. It has also been an inspired combination for, apart from sharing a respect and passion for Nat Gonella and his music, we both have interests in areas of show-business and jazz that encompass the many facets of Gonella's long and varied career.

I count myself fortunate in being a child of the 1930s, for I was able to savour the golden years of the great British dance bands and later witness the post-war revival of traditional jazz in this country. I was also able to indulge a second passion through weekly visits to variety theatres in and around London where, from a lofty perch in the 'gods', I was privileged to see many of the greatest names in entertainment, including Nat Gonella.

In 1977 I first met the man who until then I had heard only on records or seen in a stage spotlight. Over the following twenty-one years I became a regular visitor to the Gonella home as a close friend of Nat and his wife Dorothy. I rate my proudest literary achievement as 'helping to bring Nat Gonella back from the dead'. For, although Nat was only in his late sixties when the first articles were published, most people thought that he had died years before. This was understandable for, even though he had been a professional musician and entertainer from the age of sixteen, his career had reached a temporary halt.

Digby Fairweather was first struck by the Gonella bug in his formative jazz years after retrieving a record of Nat Gonella and his Georgians from the bottom of a pile of dusty 78 rpms in an antique shop. As his career as a jazz musician has progressed, Digby has never lost his passion for the unique Gonella trumpet sound and style. He realised a dream when he met his idol in the early 1980s and formed a friendship that was to last until Nat's death in 1998. With his Half-Dozen, Digby was proud to present and accompany Nat for a week of nightly appearances at London's Pizza on the Park and was also featured on Gonella's last commercial recording in February 1998. Six months later he played the cornet and led the band, and read the eulogy, at Nat's funeral.

And so, please read on and hopefully enjoy the first complete biography of Nat Gonella – British jazz pioneer and trumpeter supreme.

Ron Brown
Stubbington
March 2005

Digby Fairweather adds

Thanks to Ron Brown for his kind words. Without his original biography, *Georgia on My Mind*, this expanded and updated life story of Nat Gonella could not have become a reality. I am proud to continue to be associated with the life of this great jazzman, his loveable and down-to-earth personality — and, of course, his marvellous trumpet-playing. Ron and I hope that our book brings fond memories to old friends and fans and inspires future generations of jazz-lovers and jazz musicians to re-appreciate the work of a true British jazz pioneer. Happy reading!

Acknowledgements

We are grateful to the many people who have supported the preparation of this book or provided information. It is not possible to mention everyone by name but contributions are acknowledged in the text where possible and we apologise for any omissions. We want particularly to acknowledge the contributions of Dave Bennett, Cyril Brown, Lennie Bush, Beryl Bryden, Jim Byrne, John Chilton, Eddie Cook, Jack Fallon, Lennie Hastings, Chris Hayes, Jack Higgins, Horst Lange, Teddy Layton, Tommy McQuater, Monty Montgomery, Bill Pertwee, John Pittard, Lyman Potts, Pat Smuts, Joyce Stone, Richard M. Sudhalter, Albert Torrance, Chris Walker, Doug and Dory Whitfield, Pat and Tony Wing, Charlie Winter, Tiny Winters and John and Anna Wortham. We are grateful also to Sheila Tracey for her generous permission to quote from her book *Talking Swing: The British Big Bands*, Mainstream

Publishing, 1997, and for the support and information we received from Nat and Dorothy Gonella.

We wish to thank David Nathan of the National Jazz Archive for his help and to acknowledge the use made of the Archive and the following publications: *Jazz Journal International*, *Memory Lane*, *Popular Music Weekly* 1924-38, *Rhythm* 1936-39, *The Nat Gonella Fan Club Magazine* 1936, *Who's Who in Variety* 1946, *Radio Pictorial* 1936-1939, *Modern Style Trumpet Playing* by Nat Gonella 1935, *The Times*, *Daily Telegraph*, *Daily Mail*, *Evening News* (Portsmouth), *Portsmouth News*, *Evening Standard*, *Daily News* (New South Wales), *Melody Maker* 1934—1939, *Rhythm On Record* by Hilton R. Schleman 1936, *Band Leaders* by Julien Vedey 1950, *Louis* by Max Jones and John Chilton, and *Who's Who of British Jazz* by John Chilton, plus record catalogues and theatre programmes from the authors' collections.

Most of the photographs are from the Nat Gonella collection and the authors' collections; others were kindly provided by Natalie Wilson, Beryl Bryden, David Kenten, Malcolm Macdonald, Ian Powell, Wout Meppelink, Foto Bormann, and the *Portsmouth News*.

Ron Brown wishes to acknowledge the contribution of his wife Jan in the preparation of this book, Digby Fairweather wants to thank Lisa Bridgey and both authors are grateful to Humphrey Lyttelton for his preface and Natalie Wilson for her support.

1.

*All God's Children Got Rhythm**

Nat Gonella never shrank from the necessary self-publicity and when he hit town in the mid-1930s, everyone knew. When the Georgians arrived, it was in a small platoon of matching white limousines. Bandleader Jack Payne had a fleet of no fewer than fifteen cars; many other leaders did the same in the golden dance band years, car dealers being happy to supply new vehicles free in exchange for publicity. The Georgians' chosen venue would display a twelve-foot-high placard of their leader on the theatre fascia in his famous Parlophone pose: brandishing a trumpet, one knee held forward and wearing a striped blazer. He also had a life-size cut-out of himself displayed in every foyer, and local press photographers took great delight in photographing artist and model side by side.

Motor cars were a Gonella passion. He loved sports models and one pride and joy was his 1935 Alvis Speed-Twenty, complete with spare tyre strapped to the running-board and 'Georgia 1' painted proudly across its bonnet. At a showroom

*Parlophone, Nat Gonella and his Georgians, 19.7.1937

price of £598 there were very few such cars to be seen on the road, especially as to tax them cost a month's wages – twelve pounds fifteen shillings – for those lucky enough to have a job. Crowds would gather around the vehicle wherever it was parked, in the hope of meeting its famous owner.

The musician who received this acclaim had been born in very poor circumstances in London less than thirty years earlier. Brought up in the rough and tough district around Kings Cross – an area Gonella later described as one 'where the inhabitants eat their young' – he recalled playing in the streets with neighbourhood children when motor vehicles of any sort were still a comparative rarity. Along with the other Battle Bridge urchins Nat enjoyed the pranks of London boyhood: swinging on gas-lamp posts, and banging neighbours' door-knockers before running off. But the Caledonian Road offered distractions for a young boy at that time, including a big cattle market. Regularly the road took on the appearance of a Wild West town, with cows and sheep herded back and forth through the streets. And railway lines were never far away; smoke-belching iron giants moved constantly in and out of Kings Cross station.

The hit song of 1908, the year in which Nat Gonella was born, was 'Oh, Oh, Antonio'; *The Merry Widow* was drawing large audiences to Daley's Theatre, heavyweight boxing champion Jack Johnson knocked out 'great white hope' Tommy Burns, Winston Churchill married Clementine, and Wolverhampton Wanderers won the FA Cup. But in Islington, London, the most momentous day for the Gonella family was 7 March when their newest child bellowed his way into the world; a boy, to be named Nathaniel Charles. Children born in 1908 were known as 'Gladiator' boys or girls; a reference to the sea disaster of that year when H.M.S. *Gladiator* collided with the American liner *St Paul* off the Isle of Wight in a freak snowstorm. Nathaniel Gonella would earn his title as 'Gladiator boy': it was a suitable label for the fearless hot trumpet player he was to become.

In show business there are few performers lucky enough to have been born with a name that looks good on a poster, or in lights outside a theatre. An aspiring star can begin life as Marion Morrison and end it as John Wayne; Spangler Arlington Brough can turn into Robert Taylor, or Frances Gumm into Judy Garland. Nat Gonella clearly had no such problems. Although the Gonella family had lived in Britain for generations, the surname can be traced back to fifteenth-century Italy. Nat told a romantic story, passed down through his family for centuries, concerning a jester named Gonella in the court of nobleman Nicolo d'Este. Gonella was one of Italy's two principal jesters of the period; a second, Arlotto, was well-known for a refined sense of wit. Gonella, however, favoured cruder humour and enjoyed a reputation for practical joking. At one point he upset his master, who banished his jester with the command: 'Never tread my soil again!' Gonella retired to another province – but only long enough to dig up some earth, with which he lined his boots. Then, displaying remarkable courage, he returned to his old employer and, when challenged, emptied a boot to prove that he was indeed not treading on his master's soil. D'Este admired the jester's initiative but, deciding to play a joke of his own, he ordered Gonella's execution. His plan was that, as the jester's head was placed on the block, his executioner would pour a jug of cold water over the back of his victim's neck but the trick misfired: when the water hit the back of Gonella's blindfold head he suffered a heart attack and died of shock.

Four hundred years later, in Victorian London, Nat's grandfather, Joseph Gonella, scraped a living by playing the banjo and bones and was officially described as a 'street minstrel' as well as working in a blackface minstrel troupe. Nat could also claim a remote relationship with a third entertainer: G. H. Chirgwin – 'The White-Eyed Kaffir' – who similarly appeared for stage purposes in blackface, one eye picked out in a diamond of white greasepaint. This startling stage image was said to have been adopted after Chirgwin accidentally wiped the perspiration from around one eye one warm evening in his dressing room, and – not having time to repair the smudge – went on-stage regardless. For the rest of his career, audiences expected him to appear with this peculiar make-up as he sang his two signature songs: 'The Blind Boy' and 'My Fiddle Is My Sweetheart'.

Street-minstrel Joseph Gonella married one Emma Cobb, and they set up home in St Pancras. Their son, Richard Gonella, born in 1871, earned his living tending and riding horses, and later working as a cab driver. In due course he courted Elizabeth Finnes, who also had links with the carriage trade through her father, Nathaniel. Richard and Elizabeth were married in 1897 at All Saints Church, Kings Cross, and set up home in Islington's Edward Square, a block of tenements in the Caledonian Road. In the years to come Elizabeth would give birth to seven children. The first four were all born prior to 1908. The eldest son, Richard, was named after his father; a second child died young, but a third appears to have survived (in the early 1980s Digby Fairweather met a Victor Gonella who claimed to be this brother, but the claim is unsubstantiated). A daughter, Jessie, was born around 1906. This was a rapidly growing brood and life was far from easy, although the Gonellas were better off than some, since Richard was working at least.

After Nat's birth in 1908, the family continued to grow. In 1911, Adolphus James was born, to be followed in 1913 by Elizabeth Susan (named after her mother and known initially as 'Liz' then later as 'Lilly'). The Gonellas moved from 15 Edward Square to larger accommodation at number 22 and things showed signs of improving for the family: Richard had made the transition from driving a horse-drawn carriage to a motor cab. When Nat was seven, however, a tragic setback occurred. His father became ill and despite the efforts of Dr Beardmore, a local physician, and wife Elizabeth's increasingly desperate nursing, he died from pulmonary tuberculosis on 27 September 1915, only forty-four-years-old. Without its chief provider, the Gonella family was now in dire financial straits. Their eldest son was the only family member old enough to take on work, but the few shillings from his wages did not go very far.

Fortunately at that time charitable institutions frequently came to the aid of a family in distress. In the case of the Gonellas, the Islington Board of Guardians approached Elizabeth with a view to placing all her children, apart from her eldest son, in an orphanage. Elizabeth was distraught, but in the end agreed to release three of her youngest children into care. These included Nat and his younger brother Adolphus James, known as 'Bruts' – the nickname was said to be Nat's invention but Bruts is a semi-conventional diminution of Brother, just as Muds can be for mother, and it would stay with its owner through his own life as a trumpeter. Elder sister Jessie accompanied the boys, leaving her baby sister Elizabeth at home with her mother.

The three children were taken to St Mary's Guardians' School in Hornsey Road, north London, where they stayed for the rest of their childhood. Their new home had once been a workhouse but beneath its grim exterior the children in its charge were respected and well cared for. Although he would not live in his family home for eight more years, Nat would later be grateful for his time at St Mary's. He never went hungry, he was taught to keep himself clean and tidy and in general lived in conditions which contrasted dramatically with the daily struggle for existence at Kings Cross. Later, he would claim that any success he enjoyed in life was due largely to his upbringing in the school.

Boys and girls alike had regular lessons but, unlike many such institutions, St Mary's emphasised teaching its pupils a trade which would stand them in good stead when it was time to leave. The school was a self-contained community with classrooms, workshops, dormitories, kitchens, laundry and an infirmary where pupils received regular health checks from a doctor and dentist. Young Nat Gonella may not have been academically bright, but from his early days at school he showed an aptitude for carpentry and his teacher – although elderly and with a tendency to deafness – encouraged the fair-haired boy at every opportunity.

Carpentry, however, took second place to his love of football. Nat nourished a dream that one day he would play for his favourite team, Tottenham Hotspur, the north London club he would support for life. When he first entered St Mary's in 1915 the school boasted an excellent football team which had recently won several championship cups in north London, but several key players were about to leave. To his delight, the small but 'fast on the wing' Gonella was conscripted into the team, which practised on an asphalt pitch not more than fifty yards long. Consequently, at their first away game at Finsbury Park, the full-length pitch seemed enormous, and the St Mary's boys were soundly beaten fourteen goals to one. Worse was to come: that season they failed to win a single match! If points could have been awarded for smartest turnout, however, their school might have topped the league: their kit was the pride of the school laundry service, and the boys themselves cleaned and greased their boots to a gleaming shine.

Pride in clothing was not confined to football. St Mary's school uniform comprised neat grey suits with short trousers and, once a month, pupils were required to look their best for visiting days. Elizabeth Gonella would visit Hornsey without fail to see her three youngest children. Despite such comforting visits, however, homesick youngsters would sometimes run away from school. Nat tried this once with a friend, George Latimer, but the boys did not get far and soon found themselves held at a north London police station. The school was notified and one of the teaching staff, a Mr Whitworth, was detailed to collect them. They were ominously instructed to remove their braces and marched back to St Mary's, hands in pockets holding up their trousers. On arrival they were taken to the headmaster, George Johnson, who ordered them to take their hands out of their pockets – an inevitable preliminary to the punishment that followed.

St Mary's was also proud of its brass band. Every morning its musicians played a rousing march as the children assembled in the dining hall for breakfast, and the band was in demand for local fetes and garden parties. A highlight of the school year came when the pupils – led by the band in their resplendent uniforms of green with gold braid – marched to a local church for a harvest festival service.

The band's teacher and driving force was William Clarke, formerly of Kneller Hall and Bandmaster of the 1st East Sussex Regiment. A superb musician, Clarke knew all about brass band instruments and how to play them. And at nine years of age Nat Gonella felt ready to join his school band, although it was not altogether the music that attracted him. He told Digby Fairweather: 'I wanted the uniform! I liked the uniform more than anything!' Band rehearsals were held every weekday evening and any lad who wanted to learn an instrument was encouraged to attend an interview. 'When I first applied to get in the band,' Nat told Fairweather in 1992, 'the bandmaster said, "Well, you'd better come back in six months time." So when I went back in six months he said, "Well, try and blow this cornet." So I tried to blow my brains out! And he said, "Well, get on the drum!" So he taught me to play the drum – side-drum. Then I sort of picked up music quite quickly, and that's where I got through to join the band, by reading the music. So then he took me off the drum and taught me the cornet.'

A senior pupil, Steve Hayward, was delegated to take the aspiring young player under his wing and the two boys could often be found sitting on the stairs outside the bandroom practising their instruments together. Hayward had been abandoned as a baby and had no known relatives so, like fellow orphans at St Mary's, he had the job of meeting visitors at the school gates to take them to their waiting children. This was a job he enjoyed, as a *pourboire* – a penny or a sweet – often followed on.

Nat's progress with the cornet was rapid. William Clarke advocated the non-pressure system: the principle of blowing the cornet easily and naturally, rather than hard. This was a method Nat later passed on in his book *Modern Style Trumpet Playing*. But despite the fact that the trumpet mouthpiece is usually placed at or very near the centre of the player's lips, forming an orthodox embouchure, Nat Gonella, for almost all of his performing career, played from the side of his mouth.

This unusual method developed while he was troubled by cold sores and a split lip at St Mary's in winter. In his trumpet tutor Nat explained the problem for himself:

> At an early stage in my career when I had to do a considerable amount of playing without any chance of resting, I suffered from a split lip which refused to heal no matter what I did – which was everything except the obvious remedy of rest. The split was in the dead-centre of my lip where normally I placed my mouthpiece and was caused no doubt by the fact that I had not even heard of the non-pressure system at that time. [So] I contrived to get along by blowing out of the side of my mouth – away from the split. Gradually I learned to make do, and when I added the non-pressure system I found it easier to stay where I was.

In the interim, William Clarke tried to persuade his pupil to play centrally, but in the end conceded that a side embouchure suited the boy better and produced admirable results. In later years, after Nat had become an established trumpet star, some up-and-coming trumpeters emulated his method causing him great amusement. 'I positively blush with shame,' he wrote in his tutor book, 'when I think of the many trumpet players who have paid me the compliment of imitation. They are, of course, utterly wrong to do so!' Clearly, though, Nat was showing enough promise at this point for his academically trained teacher to bend orthodox rules on his account when brass playing was still a high discipline. And occasionally today trumpeters play on the side: Brian Rankin of the BBC Big Band is an example, as is Digby Fairweather.

Every member of the school band was taught to read music as a matter of course; their repertoire comprised light classical and standard brass band pieces. Legitimate instrumental training was similarly taken for granted. 'They taught me how to play the cornet,' Nat told Fairweather in 1992. 'I had to learn it properly, triple-tonguing and everything. We played overtures, the marches. We didn't play any dance music. Strictly classical!' Nevertheless, like Nat, several of his fellow pupils later used their training in prominent dance bands. His friend George Latimer, who took up the trombone at the school, later enjoyed a successful career, and brothers Sid and Ernie Fearn were destined to play in trumpet sections under Jack Payne and Billy Cotton respectively. Bruts Gonella ultimately graduated from St Mary's brass band to work with Billy Cotton and Lew Stone as well as Nat's Georgians.

With such talent in the ranks, St Mary's band was better than most, entering three major band contests and placing in all of them. Third prize at a contest in Tufnell Park was followed by a return one year later to take the first. The most prestigious award of all, however, took place at Crystal Palace, where the band was awarded third place in the junior section of a major contest.

When Nat, Bruts and Jessie arrived at St Mary's, the First World War was in its second year, bringing a first terrifying experience of air raids. Nat remembered an aerial torpedo exploding 150 yards down the road, shattering every window in the school. Another victim was a nearby public house, the Eaglet, where many lives were lost.

By the time Nat was thirteen he was, in his own phrase, 'something of a big shot'; head boy, captain of the football team, sergeant of the school band, and the winner of awards for his carpentry and in the school boxing championship. His account of this last victory was modest. His opponent, much bigger than he was, looked the likely winner within seconds of the start of the bout. In sheer desperation, Nat struck out and happened to catch his unlucky antagonist on the nose; the bleeding would not stop and the lucky survivor was awarded a technical knockout!

Just as everything was going well, however, Gonella's hopes for the future were severely threatened by rheumatic fever; after coming near to death he was confined to bed in the school's hospital for six months. On recovery, he was told that the illness had left him with a weak heart and that any strenuous activities – from football to playing the cornet – were now dangerous. William Clarke suggested that he might take up two less taxing instruments: the E-flat tenor horn and the violin. Later Nat would play violin briefly in Bob Dryden's band, but his main progress was on the tenor horn, and within months of adopting the instrument he won the soloist's prize at a north London band contest.

At age fifteen, Nat Gonella would leave St Mary's for good. Many ex-bandsmen went straight into the army (as their training intended) and – once again attracted by a uniform – Nat hoped to join the 15th Hussars. Presenting himself at the regiment's Westminster recruiting office, the would-be recruit stood only five foot three inches tall, and weighed nine stone ten pounds. But he was tough and wiry and confident that he would sail through the medical which ensued. No such thing, however. The medical officer detected a weak heart and Nat was brusquely informed that the army would not require his services. Strangely enough, eighteen years on, all such decisions were forgotten and Nat Gonella was called up and into the army for the Second World War. For now, though, denied even a carpenter's training at St Mary's (for similar medical reasons), what was he to do? Once again his school came to the rescue. With only a few months to go until his departure, Nat was hastily taught the rudiments of tailoring, and by his last week at school had mastered the art of fashioning button-holes.

When the day arrived for Nat to bid farewell to Bruts, Jessie, William Clarke, his principal, teachers and friends, he did so with a heavy heart. St Mary's had been his home for eight years and had provided a training which would stand him in good stead. Instilled in him were stout measures of independence and self-preservation as well as the most important lifetime's gift of all – an introduction to music.

2

*Blow That Horn!**

The employment department at St Mary's worked hard to ensure that its young charges should get as good a start to their working lives as possible, and finding decent jobs for them was a top priority. Because of his coronary complications Nat was one of its more difficult challenges, but after much searching a position was secured for him at a London tailoring firm in Albany Street, close to Regents Park.

But where was he to live? In partnership with the Guardians' school there was a hostel for ex-pupils and, as many had no families, this was a second welcome haven. House rules were strict, however. On receiving pay packets at the end of the week, the young guests handed them to the hostel manager, who – after deducting money for food and board – divided the remainder between the wage-earner and any parents and dependants. Bedtimes were strictly observed, and church attendance on Sundays was compulsory.

Nat opted for the hostel, and from it set off for a first day of

*Parlophone, Nat Gonella and his Georgians, 9.3.37

work as a tailor's apprentice, stitching lapels. A second, then a third day followed, and the tedious sojourn was more than enough to convince him that he was not cut out for the job. He duly handed in his needle and thread, collecting six shillings for this short career in the rag trade. 'I could never have made a tailor,' he would joke in later years. 'I couldn't sit cross-legged for long enough!'

The decision was unwelcome at the hostel, but Nat found himself another job almost at once. In Great Portland Street he was struck by a sign outside a furrier's: 'Wanted – errand boy!' Polishing the toecaps of his shoes on the legs of his trousers, he went in to see if the post was still available. It was, and he was offered the job at the wage of fifteen shillings a week. From this sum his hostel retained ten shillings for board and lodgings; his mother received two shillings and sixpence, while Nat retained the remaining half-a-crown for personal pleasures. But he was happy with the new job; his employer treated him kindly and he was free to travel about in London by bus or tram.

Nat's errand boy duties were not without moments of minor drama: one day he was told to deliver an expensive fur to a large Regent Street store by bus. It was a fine day and, engrossed in looking out at the West End from an upstairs seat, it was only at the last moment that he realised he had reached his stop. Leaping down the stairs he jumped off the vehicle as it moved away, only to remember that he had left his valuable parcel behind in the luggage rack under the stairs. Nat was quick to calculate that at a wage of fifteen shillings a week it would take him a very long time indeed to pay back the money for a lost fur coat. Panic-stricken, he ran across Piccadilly Circus to cut off the bus, momentarily caught in heavy traffic around Eros island, and leaping on the running-board retrieved his precious cargo, holding it close to him until the bus drew to a halt again.

Despite such youthful mishaps, the errand boy quickly settled into his new job, and soon received a pay-rise to eighteen shillings. This persuaded him to leave the hostel and return home to his mother; the extra money would help the family.

By this time the Gonellas had moved to George's Road, Upper Holloway, a few streets away from the Caledonian Market. This was a typical working-class district of 1920s London: rows of terrace houses with front doors leading directly from the pavement into gloomy overcrowded dwellings. Like many others, George's Road was a self-contained community in which small shops catered for neighbours, offering the bonus of 'goods on the slate until the weekend'. These included Ernie Popple's bakery, Mansi's fruit and vegetables, a sweetshop run by Ed Aimes, and barber Jim Ellis where Nat regularly requested 'short back and sides'. The road also boasted five pubs and alehouses. Sixty years later, when Ron Brown visited George's Road to find out if it had changed, the tiny terrace houses had made way for a large housing estate with multi-storey flats. Only one pub remained; originally the Royal Victory, it had changed its name in 1982 to the Moynahan Arms. It has now closed.

Returning to his family, Nat was forcibly reminded of the good value his subsidised hostel life had offered. Back home it was a struggle to survive, but Elizabeth Gonella had taken a small job and her family chipped in as best they could.

On 28 November 1923 a momentous musical event would change Nat Gonella's life forever. Delivering a boxed item to a customer down Union Street, his eyes were drawn across the road to the windows of a large music store. A sign proclaimed

'Rudd and Company – Manufacturers and Importers of Pianofortes and Harmoniums', but what Nat saw in the window was a shining cornet. The instrument was second-hand but in good condition, and he gazed at it for some minutes, trying to ignore its price-tag marked three pounds ten shillings, a small fortune when set against the money he was left with after handing the best part of his wage packet to his mother. With one last longing look he hurried off to make his next delivery.

At the end of his working day, Nat went home in a state of semi-concealed excitement to his mother who could see her son had urgent matters on his mind. Eventually Nat told her the story. Elizabeth Gonella listened sympathetically, and after some thought suggested that the instrument might be bought 'on terms'. Next day Nat hurried back to Union Street, noting with relief that the cornet was still in the window, and went in to take a closer look. From behind his counter the salesman studied the fair-haired young man gazing lovingly at the instrument. Then, crossing to the window, he lifted out the cornet and handed it to him. Nat set it to his lips and – much to the dealer's amazement – blew a note-perfect rendition of 'Yes We Have No Bananas!' Realising that this was a talented young player, the proprietor listened to his request and then – after some gentle bargaining – settled on an offer. Nat would put five shillings down and pay off the balance at half-a-crown a week. With a six-month contract finally sealed, the errand boy left the shop, the proud owner of his very first cornet.

It was not until he reached home and went to his bedroom to practise that he remembered his doctor's warning of two years previously. But the urge to play was strong and soon it was clear there was no cause for concern. In fact the rest had lent new zest and strength to the young cornettist's playing and soon it was ringing round his street. At this time, long before radio and television, families regularly entertained themselves with home-produced music. Friends and relatives would visit at weekends for a sing-song and if a crate of brown ale should be on hand all the better! As word spread about Nat's playing he was soon in demand for parties and musical evenings, and even took his cornet to work at the furrier's to entertain the staff when seniors were out of the way.

Around this time, Nat was approached by the director of the St Pancras British Legion Brass Band and, once again, the promise of a smart new uniform proved irresistible: he presented himself twice a week for rehearsals. The band was popular around north London and most Sunday mornings could be heard playing free concerts on the bandstand at the foot of Parliament Hill. Afterwards, bandsmen would adjourn to the nearest pub; Nat would tag along and usually a glass of lemonade and an arrowroot biscuit would be passed his way. With the Legion band he made his paid professional debut, playing at an up-market Hampstead garden party. Happy to be back making music, he was gaining experience. Reading music again, playing in a section and blowing into the open air all constituted valuable grounding.

Every Friday, back in the furrier's workshop, a star-struck girl who worked alongside Nat religiously bought and scanned *The Stage*, even then a renowned source of show-business opportunities. During a pre-weekend tea break she pointed out an advertisement to Nat. 'Wanted,' it read, 'young boys, 16–18, who play brass instruments. Apply: Archie Pitt.' A contact address was included, in City Road. Nat was apprehensive – this looked like the big time – but, encouraged by his workmates, he decided to answer the call. Consequently a plan was laid: he would set off on a fictitious errand on Saturday morning and visit Mr Pitt instead.

Unfortunately, on that Saturday morning, Nat found himself at the wrong end of City Road and had to trudge back to the Angel, Islington, to reach his destination. There, with an unseen band audible nearby, he reported to a Miss Freeman who – discovering that the young visitor had not brought his cornet with him – retrieved one from a member of the unseen band and handed it to him with the blunt request: 'Play something'. Nat obliged with a favourite march theme from the British Legion band's repertoire and Miss Freeman, with no visible signs of enthusiasm, asked him to come back that afternoon, this time with his cornet.

Back at the furrier's it was Saturday half-day closing, but by losing himself in City Road and the subsequent delays Nat arrived back at work three hours later than expected. His employer's daughter, awaiting the absentee with a face like thunder, administered a severe reprimand and told him to expect the sack, come Monday. But at that moment Nat Gonella was none too worried; all he could think about was getting home to collect his cornet as quickly as possible, then making for his afternoon's audition. Arriving back at City Road, he was ushered into the company of nine more boys: the junior band he had heard earlier. With them, Nat played a march, a faultless performance which, this time, appeared to satisfy the stoical Miss Freeman. 'Go down to Alhambra Theatre in Leicester Square,' she instructed him. 'Mr Pitt – Mr Archie Pitt – will be waiting for you.'

This posed a problem. Nat wanted to look smart, but owned only one tattered suit. By now, though, he was determined to make an impression on Archie Pitt and get the job. So, dusting off his suit jacket as best he could he donned the uniform trousers of his Legion band and, satisfied that he was as presentable as current finances would allow, hurried to the Alhambra.

Although he may have wondered why the young man before him was wearing blue trousers with a gold stripe and a faded grey jacket, Archie Pitt was charming, asking Nat about his present job, his family and musical experience. Then, after a ten-minute exchange, and satisfied with what he heard, he offered his interviewee three pounds a week to join the boys' band he was forming for a lengthy tour of variety halls. This was big money indeed and Nat accepted on the spot. 'You'll have to sign a contract,' Pitt reminded him, 'for which your mother must be present. Oh, and I want you to start on Monday with us. If you can't leave your job that quickly, then you can rehearse with us every evening next week and start the Monday after.'

On the Monday morning following, Nat arrived at his place of work early to break the news, first to the stage-struck girl who had begun it all and then to his workmates. Soon afterwards he was called to the office for the predicted reprimand and possible dismissal and, treating attack as the best form of defence, handed in his notice immediately. When his employer learned about Nat's show-business hopes, however, the older man was understanding. After all, he had stood as Nat's guarantor for the purchase of his cornet in the first place. 'Good luck for the future,' he said. 'And you can leave at the end of the week.'

The week over, Gonella's professional career began. Everything was new and exciting. Archie Pitt's juvenile band, the Busby Boys, had been formed for a brand-new production but, in order to prepare his young players for the rigours of stage-work and touring, Pitt had arranged for them to travel –

though not to play – with his current presentation, which was just coming off tour. The show – *Mr Tower of London* – had been a success and brought to prominence Pitt's wife, Gracie Fields, in the role of Sally Perkins. Pitt and Fields had married in 1923, for business as much as for love, but the role he had created for her was ideal for any aspiring young actress (later, in the 1930s, it was taken over with notable success by Betty Driver of *Coronation Street* fame). When *Mr Tower of London* finished its run, Pitt's juveniles began rehearsals at Alexandra Palace for his new show, *A Week's Pleasure*, and just before the opening it was decided that trumpets rather than cornets would look better for stage purposes. Accordingly, Nat was presented with his first full-length B-flat trumpet.

Opening night arrived and *A Week's Pleasure* was hailed as another triumph. The new show was even more of a family affair: though Gracie Fields confined herself to choreography and stage-managing her juvenile band, her sister, Betty, played the lead in the show and Edith and Tommy Fields were also in the cast. And Archie Pitt's Busby Boys – five trumpets, two tenor horns, two trombones, one saxophone, euphonium, sousaphone and drums – created a nightly sensation. Later, juvenile bands became a popular and familiar show-business phenomenon, but the Busby Boys were among the first of their kind. Their repertoire included light classics ('Poet and Peasant' and 'Light Cavalry') and popular songs of the day, including 'Ukulele Lady' and 'The Sheik of Araby'. One of the highlights of the show was their 'Guardsmen' routine: each boy was resplendent in a bright red tunic dripping with gold braid and topped with a busby. Young Nat Gonella may have been a newcomer to show business but he savoured the applause night after night and knew instantly that he had found his life's vocation: to play the trumpet and entertain.

Archie Pitt was pleased with what he saw and heard too; *A Week's Pleasure* toured all the best theatres in Britain and within two weeks he had raised the wages of each Busby Boy to three pounds five shillings a week. Fifteen shillings were put into an individual bank account for each member and part of the remainder sent home, no doubt to grateful parents.

Six weeks into the tour the show changed musical directors. The new arrival was a fine musician, Bert Gutsell, who later – under the more romantic name of 'Bertini' – led Blackpool's renowned Tower Ballroom Orchestra. Back in 1924, however, Gutsell had his work cut out to control an ensemble of high-spirited teenage boys. To his credit he entered into the spirit of things, arranging cricket and football matches for his young charges when rehearsals were over. Unrepentantly however, they engaged in pranks and mischief, usually punished by a fine from Archie Pitt.

Several members of the Busby Boys went on to distinguished careers in dance music and jazz. Max Abrams, one of Britain's best-known drummers (and later teachers) and a long-time friend of Nat Gonella, had a premier career with Jack Hylton, Carroll Gibbons and his Savoy Orpheans, Geraldo, Ambrose, Jack Payne, Sid Phillips and many other famous names. Trumpeter Freddy Wood went on to join Bertini at Blackpool Tower, and later still became a cornerman of 'Big Bill' Campbell's Rocky Mountaineers. Although Nat Gonella became the Busby Boys' first trumpet, when he first joined the band Freddy Wood was playing lead. Another Busby Boy trumpeter, Johnny Morrison, later joined a number of well-known bands, and after Nat formed his Georgians worked as their stage-manager before leaving to work on cruise-liners. And Nat's brother Bruts, who joined the Busby Boys directly from St Mary's Guardian School had a long, successful career as a trumpter.

The Busby Boys' routines were an integral part of *A Week's Pleasure*. In addition to playing music, they were required to perform song-and-dance acts and were coached every morning in singing and tap-dancing; Nat Gonella even learned to do the splits. Gracie Fields took a genuine interest in their welfare, especially as several members were away from home and family for the first time in their lives. Having spent much of his childhood in an orphanage, Nat had overcome the pain of such insecurities long before, but he still enjoyed taking part in outings arranged by Fields. And if the show was playing a week's season she hired bicycles for the boys so that, for a few hours, they could escape from the stuffy atmosphere of theatre and rehearsal rooms.

Gracie took a special liking to the cherubic-featured Nat, realising that he had both enthusiasm and a talent for the popular tunes of the day rather than the light classics he often played on-stage. There was even a suggestion that the two of them should collaborate on a jazzy selection called 'Doo Wacka Doo!' but this never materialised. It was Gracie nevertheless who introduced Nat to jazz. One day she gave him an old Decca wind-up gramophone which she had replaced for herself with a newer model, plus half a dozen records. These featured the 'Denza Dance Band', a title attached to various groups recorded by Columbia between 1925 and 1927 and including both British and American combinations. Most of the British recordings were made by contingents from the Savoy Orpheans and Savoy Havana Band, but the American sides were something else again, including such talents as Frank Trumbauer, Adrian Rollini, Red Nichols, Miff Mole, Eddie Lang and Bix Beiderbecke. When Nat heard the round-ed chime of Beiderbecke's cornet he was immediately captivated by the sound, and intrigued by the way that Bix's improvisations travelled this way then that – the new phenomenon called jazz. Gracie Fields' gift had furnished him with an entirely new slant on the cornet and from then on he became a record fanatic, spending most of his pocket-money to add to his collection and playing his new acquisitions on the old gramophone, which travelled with him from town to town.

One day, while *A Week's Pleasure* was playing in Nottingham, Nat was standing outside a music store when a record in the window drew his attention. He was sufficiently intrigued to enter the shop and ask to hear what he had seen. The dealer laid the 78 disc on the turntable and lowered the heavy pick-up. The record was 'Cushion Foot Stomp' by Fletcher Henderson and the trumpet player was Louis Armstrong. Gonella was instantly mesmerised by Armstrong's tone and technique; never had he dreamed that the trumpet was capable of such expressiveness, power, and inspirational lift. This was to be a turning point in his career; a door opening to a great new musical landscape. Little did he realise that, soon enough, he would meet Armstrong and that they would become lifelong friends.

Gonella's newly acquired passion for jazz rapidly landed him in hot water. Whenever the Busby Boys played a popular dance tune he and Max Abrams could seldom control their urge to swing out; their hot renditions of 'The Sheik of Araby' would draw thunderous looks and a reprimand from Bert Gutsell, but always met with audience approval. Nat and Max paid only token attention to Gutsell's objections. They explored jazz at every opportunity and converted some of their fellow players too; the Busby Boys' tenor horn player even bought a saxophone to join in secret jam sessions.

Meanwhile *A Week's Pleasure* was nearing the end of its two-and-a-half-year run, and when it did the Busby Boys returned to Alexandra Palace to rehearse for a new Pitt production, *Safety First*. This new show allowed the boys more scope. They changed costume several times in order to portray cowboys and Indians, soldiers, and even the Royal Canadian Mounted Police, and were encouraged to show off their tap-dancing and to appear in comedy sketches. Nat's own favourite took place in a Western saloon. Two trumpets, trombone and drums, unfettered by Bert Gutsell, blew as they pleased, the band dressed in cowboy uniforms, complete with Stetsons and six-guns in holsters. The boys were also trained to shift scenery and, in one sketch with a nautical theme, were detailed to lie beneath a rowing boat on rockers and move it backwards and forwards to create a rocking effect. If they tired, a few sharp words from the wings encouraged them to keep going.

By now things were looking even brighter for Nat Gonella. He was promoted to 'sergeant' in the Busby Boys and his pay raised to the considerable sum of five pounds a week. Bruts Gonella, whom he had also introduced to jazz, had joined the troupe, and whenever they shared lodgings the old gramophone worked overtime. To avoid giving their hosts cause for complaint they played their records under the bedsheets using pins, not gramophone needles, to reduce the sound still further. *Safety First* was a huge success wherever it played and at the end of the season the Busby Boys confidently expected Archie Pitt to promote them in variety as a separate attraction. But this turned out not to be the case. A week before the show closed, each member unexpectedly received his notice.

After four years, Archie Pitt's Busby Boys had become a way of life and sole source of income for Nat Gonella. What would happen now?

3

*Sweet Music Man**

Safety First played its final week in Margate, Kent and, with the prospect of the labour exchange or listings in *The Stage* looming for the show's cast, the atmosphere behind the front curtain was gloomy.

On the Saturday night, with three days to go, Nat Gonella sat in the dressing room contemplating whatever future was left for him in the music world. Over the year he had been approached by several respected small-time bandleaders with offers, but could consider none of them because of his Pitt contract. This night, however, his luck was in. After the show he was told that someone wanted to talk to him; a well-wisher had been impressed by Nat's playing and knew of a local band in urgent need of a trumpeter. Might he be interested? Nat certainly was, but he realised he must move quickly. At the end of the week the unknown bandleader would have five trumpeters to choose from. So, after a second meeting with a go-between, an audition was arranged.

*Parlophone, Nat Gonella and his Georgians, 21.1.36

The leader in question was drummer Bob Dryden, whose band held the 1928 summer residency at Margate's prestigious Dreamland Ballroom. When he saw Nat making his tentative entry, the drummer's eyebrows rose. They rose further as the youngster delved into a battered case to produce an equally weather-beaten trumpet. Thinking that here was fun to be had, Dryden handed the new arrival a leadsheet for 'Swamp Blues', a jazz-based piece that would have tested any experienced trumpet player of the period. But by now Gonella was an excellent reader. Oblivious to the bemused gazes of his onlookers, he set trumpet to side-embouchure and rattled through 'Swamp Blues' with much of the confidence of a young Louis Armstrong. First impressions, Dryden was quick to admit, had been wrong and Nat Gonella was invited to join his band, starting Monday, at seven pounds a week.

After the final curtain fell on *Safety First* Nat said goodbye to his colleagues of four years. It was a sad moment; over the period he had made close friends within the band. But now, at twenty, it was time to move on into the adult world of music and he had done so without a break in his career.

Playing in a dance band was a new experience. Until this point he had been accustomed to a seated theatre audience; now he had a multitude of dancers in front of his trumpet bell. By the late 1920s Britain was experiencing what *Popular Music Weekly* described at the time as 'dancemania'. Almost every city and town could boast a dance hall and dance bands were in great demand. The Dreamland Ballroom was a prestige booking and its ten-piece band, led by Dryden from behind his drums, comprised Guy Snowden (first alto), Charlie March (second alto), Bill Tate (tenor), 'Kack' Harris (trombone), Jerry Stone (violin), Harold Patrick (piano), Albert Haydon (guitar), Jack Walter (bass), and now Nat Gonella (trumpet). There was plenty of scope for improvising, tossing choruses from player to player and experimenting with jazz, and Nat took every opportunity to indulge his growing passion for this new music.

Within the Dryden band he had a fellow jazz enthusiast. Trombonist Harris jealously guarded a collection of jazz records, including sides by Bix Beiderbecke, Red Nichols, Paul Whiteman and Louis Armstrong. Harris cleaned his records as carefully as if they were antique china but he allowed Nat to listen to them. At this point British musicians were only just becoming aware of Armstrong. Red Nichols, Miff Mole and their less passionate peers had preceded his arrival on record in Britain. But Nat Gonella latched on to Louis; Armstrong's records were quickly playing an increasingly important role in shaping both his approach and technique, and he waited impatiently for the each new title to reach the record shop.

There was one he could never forget: 'Wild Man Blues', recorded by Louis in Chicago on 4 April 1927. He had acquired it in the last months of work with Pitt and fallen in love with the record (later he re-recorded it on his autobiographical album *The Nat Gonella Story* in 1961). To learn Louis' solo note for note he played and replayed it, his early attempts falling far short of the recorded original. In his own down-to-earth words: 'It really drove me round the ruddy bend – the Armstrong range was so much higher than my own.' For a time he compromised by dropping an octave whenever Armstrong flew into the trumpet's top register. Subsequently he sent away to Darewski's music publishing company for the sheet music, eagerly scanning it when it arrived. It was only then that he realised how much improvisation Armstrong had introduced into his recorded version. Still, Nat Gonella stuck to the job and after several hard-working weeks could produce a passable paraphrase of the original. He also bought a clarinet and (remarkably) taught himself to play the instrument well enough to approximate Johnny Dodds' dramatic solo.

By the time the Margate summer season was over, Nat was a popular figure in Bob Dryden's band and had bought himself a new trumpet. The band was well liked and subsequently contracted to spend the winter at the Rivoli Ballroom in Manchester. Billed as 'Bob Dryden and His Rivoli Rhythm Boys', they were a hit and played engagements around Lancashire, enjoying celebrity treatment from local fans. One such job was a Jewish wedding, for which the Rivoli Rhythm Boys were required to play from midday until two in the morning – a formidable period, luckily interspersed with generous breaks for food and drink. By two o'clock, understandably, the latter was taking its toll. Just as the band had staggered to its feet for 'God Save the King', the MC hissed to Bob Dryden that his guests required more music and the exhausted Rhythm Boys fell back in their seats. One ungenerous rumour back in Manchester claimed that the whole band was too drunk to stand up: untrue, but at least one member finished up that way by the night's end. Fellow members propelled their unsteady colleague to the exit but, every time they left him standing alone in order to hail a taxi, down he went. Then someone had a bright idea and tied the inebriated one to a lamp post with his own dress-scarf until a cab arrived to take him to his lodgings.

It was now that Nat was introduced to the art of song-plugging by Leslie Holmes who later teamed with comedian Leslie Sarony to form 'The Two Leslies', a successful comedy duo. Holmes was working for Campbell Connelly and Co., music publishers, and spent many hours singing their new songs with the Dryden band, who later adopted the same practice for themselves. At sixpence a copy they sometimes sold as many as two hundred copies at one time, providing a useful boost to band income.

As the six-month season at the Rivoli was nearing its end, the ballroom's management asked the Rhythm Boys to stay on. Bob Dryden had other plans; he had been privately negotiating for an attractive residency in Belfast and consequently stalled his employers until it was confirmed. But there was a problem. Although terms had been agreed, his Belfast backer insisted on an audition before contracts could be signed, and so Dryden bribed the Rivoli's caretaker to open the ballroom at ten o'clock one Sunday morning so that his band could play for their employer-to-be. All went well until the Rivoli manager appeared unexpectedly and a row erupted between the three men. As it was physically impossible for him to throw all of the band out of the ballroom, the aggrieved manager decided to sabotage proceedings by closing the stage curtains and switching off all the lighting. The band continued doggedly in almost total darkness, and the backer – who took the crisis in good part – duly signed the contract for a three-month stint at the Plaza Ballroom, Belfast.

Nat enjoyed his stay in Northern Ireland. In addition to their residency at the Plaza, the Dryden band was able to take on other gigs around the area, as they had done in Manchester. Nat's experience was growing apace, but he found himself working unduly hard. In addition to the trumpet, he could also play the violin and clarinet (though his talents on the violin were, in his phrase, 'not that hot'), and as a result found himself in some section of the orchestra for everything from a waltz to a tango. Matters came to a head one night at the Plaza when, after a fierce row with Dryden, Nat smashed his violin dramatically on a nearby table. As the astonished musicians surveyed the mangled remains, Nat calmly observed: 'Well –

that finishes me in the tango section!' This was a drastic demonstration; the violin had cost him nearly two pounds.

After the Dryden band completed their Irish residency they moved back to Margate for a season at the Casino Ballroom, this time as a six-piece comprising two trumpets, two saxophones, piano and drums. They had to work hard for their wages: seven pounds a week per man, playing for lunchtime, teatime and evening sessions. The year was 1929, and Nat was regularly delivering Armstrong-style vocals to the delight of patrons who were in no doubt they were hearing the very best in hot jazz. Nat was not so sure: 'pretty corny' was the way he later summarily dismissed his early vocal efforts.

The Casino Ballroom stood next to the Dreamland and Nat quickly got to know members of its new resident orchestra. They included musicians who would later become household names in the world of popular entertainment: clarinettist Nat Temple, drummer Maurice Burman and Sam Costa – still working as a pianist before his successful future career as singer, comedian and broadcaster. All these young stars would drop in to the Casino to hear Nat Gonella play.

But during his summer season at Margate the young trumpeter became restless. He was happy and doing well with Bob Dryden, but felt it was time for a change. His growing reputation as trumpeter and singer had already prompted several offers from other local bandleaders. But it was after following up an advertisement in *Melody Maker* that he opted to move along the coast to Brighton. The move was made to join Archie Alexander's band which held the residency at Brighton's Regent Ballroom, an entertainment centre offering cinema and dance-hall facilities and attracting both locals and holiday-makers. The proprietors had powerful London connections too; they owned Wimbledon's Palais de Dance and the Canadian Palais de Dance in Tottenham. Alexander himself was a keen jazz fan and gave his new trumpeter free rein to play selections that Nat had laboriously transcribed by hand from records, including Armstrong's 'West End Blues' and Eddie Lang's 'Freeze and Melt' and 'Bugle Call Rag'. Aside from this, Nat also acted as stooge for a comedy act introduced to break up the music. It was all good experience for the trumpeter, but he was still working hard, playing two sessions a day, every day including weekends, for seven pounds a week.

Bruts Gonella, unlike his brother, had found himself jobless after the break-up of Archie Pitt's Busby Boys, two years before, in 1928. By this time – while his brother starred at the Regent – Bruts was also working in Brighton, but as a messenger at the Metropole Hotel on the seafront. He managed to find evening jobs around the area and subsequently joined the resident band at Sherry's Ballroom, Brighton.

During his Brighton stay Nat was to meet with at least two more major life opportunities, the first of them at a coffee stall where entertainers gathered late in the evening to wind down after the show. One night, sipping his coffee, he fell into conversation with a glamorous hostess from Sherry's, Betty Godecharle, and within three months – in the spring of 1930 – she and Nat were married in Wandsworth, London. On her twenty-second birthday in October 1930, Betty gave birth to a daughter, Natalie. 'Betty, my mother, was such a glamorous soul,' she remembered in late 2002, 'always dripping in furs and it was always, "Oh my darling Natalie." Very well educated, well spoken and vivacious.' But mother and father were both just twenty-two-years-old. 'So very young,' Natalie observed, 'to cope with all that was happening to them.' The marriage would last only seven years.

It was in Brighton too that Gonella first met someone who

would become a regular colleague in the thirties, clarinettist/saxophonist Albert Torrance. Still living in central London, Torrance told Digby Fairweather in 2004:

> Nat was playing for Archie Alexander and now and then I used to go and play there a bit, because I was very much an amateur in those days – very, very young, and at that time studying architecture at the local college. The band was very good, even in those days, and of course Nat stood out a mile; a natural born brilliant player. But more than that, he was an instant friend of mine. He was a real genuine man; any other man would have liked to have him as a friend. He had a flat in North Street and I used to go there now and again and meet him and his wife Betty. I liked her – it's funny how it broke up. But I also knew the fellow she went off with – a great big all-in wrestler! Later on I found a photograph of Betty and sent it to Natalie, because prior to that she hadn't had any pictures of her at all and she was so pleased!

Torrance's friendship with Gonella developed during the 1930s; the trumpeter recommended the young saxophonist to Brian Lawrance, whom he joined at Quaglino's, and later to Frank Gregori, and until 1935 Torrance recorded prolifically with Gonella too. But, in his own words: 'I think that was when Nat was a wee bit angry with me. He had an engagement to go to Scandinavia and he wanted me to go with him. [But] I was getting a bit settled down with my wife – one in a million – so what was the point of going away? I had a job and I was happy. And that was when Pat Smuts joined him in the Georgians.' Torrance would continue recording regularly with Gonella however until May 1939: the Georgians' last recording session prior to the Second World War.

The final opportunity in Brighton was musical, and Gonella's biggest break so far. The town received a visit from a leading bandleader from London. Up in Archer Street, Soho

(London's legendary musicians' centre), the jungle drums had told of a sensational trumpeter down in Brighton who could play and sing just like Louis Armstrong. Could it be true? Billy Cotton came to find out.

Cotton turned up during an afternoon tea-dance at the Regent, a ballroom he already knew well, as his own London Savannah Band had been formed there for a season in 1924. Despite trying to keep his head down, the famous visitor was spotted by Archie Alexander who – keen to show off his band – handed round several of Gonella's hottest American transcriptions. This, of course, was exactly what Cotton was waiting to hear and he was impressed enough to contact Nat later, inviting him to audition for his band at London's Streatham Locarno. Nat was not slow to accept the offer: opportunities like this were thin on the ground. After a hasty visit to London and the promised audition, Nat signed a contract on the spot for eight pounds ten shillings a week (in 1930 an average working wage was less than a quarter of the sum). Just six years earlier he had left home with Archie Pitt's Busby Boys. Now, at twenty-two, he was a married man with wife Betty and a newborn daughter, Natalie, and he had fulfilled his ambition: to star in a top-line 'name' band in London.

Fellow Cockneys, he and Cotton got on well. 'Billy was very easy-going and very friendly,' Gonella told author Sheila Tracy, for her book *Talking Swing*, 'and he had other interests because he was a racing motorist. He was a man of the world, he wasn't an evening dress man, and he would mix with everybody. Very easy to get on with.' With his new leader, Nat was encouraged to develop his Armstrong impressions for featured solo spots in the band's show. For these, at the time, he wore a brown mask with holes cut for mouth and eyes and a crinkled curly wig, a minstrel device which should be viewed forgivingly in the context of its era. Cotton's band, however, its showmanship aside, was musically of premier-league quality, including Sid Buckman (trumpet) Sydney Lipton (violin), Mickey Burberry (clarinet), Joe Ferrie (trombone) and pianist/arranger Clem Bernard, as well as singer Alan Breeze whose career with Cotton spanned thirty-six years.

It was during one of his solo spots that Nat received a sharp reminder of the perils of combining playing and drinking. Just before a hot version of 'Some of These Days' he knocked back a pint of beer. All was well until the concluding trumpet 'E', a spectacular high-note finale which Nat hit but could not hold. 'When we got to the end of the number,' he told Tracy, 'there was a long, high note held for six bars and I was very confident but when I went for this note I missed it. I struggled for it again and I missed it again, and I struggled for it about three or four times and finished up with tears in my eyes as I went to sit down. That was my first experience of doing a solo out front!'

From Streatham Locarno, Billy Cotton's band moved up-market to the exclusive Ciro's Club in Orange Street. This offer apparently surprised several music papers and their pundits, for Ciro's was select and generally employed bands that provided refined musical fare only – the opposite, presumably, to Cotton's Cockney exuberance, typified by his 'wakey-wakey' trademark of later years. The club offered its patrons drinking, dining and the opportunity to exchange undisturbed small-talk and gossip while being served by waiters decked out as flunkies in satin knee-breeches and powdered periwigs. Occasionally, after sufficient intake of champagne, members of the aristocratic clientele might condescend to step on to the dance floor to give their marcel-waved partners a twirl.

Cotton and his players rapidly became depressed with the

rules of the management and the resultant need to tone their music down – particularly the jazz-inspired features of Nat Gonella. Once a week, however, things improved when the band was employed by the BBC to broadcast live from the club. This allowed Gonella and partners to raise both volume and tempo as well as giving millions of young radio listeners the opportunity to enjoy Nat's trumpet solo and vocal on 'Ain't Misbehavin'' (Armstrong's first mega-hit of the period) and other hot selections. While playing with Cotton, he also made his first records for the Regal label. As trumpeter and part of a vocal trio (completed by Cotton and Alan Breeze) he can be heard on 'That Rhythm Man!' recorded on 14 August 1930, but 'Bessie Couldn't Help It' by Hoagy Carmichael – recorded one week later on 21 October – is his first full-length vocal on record. During this second session he also supplied a short scat interlude (fourteen bars of vocal interjections, along with a full and spectacular trumpet chorus) for 'The New Tiger Rag'.

'Bessie Couldn't Help It' – a decidedly suggestive song for its time – proved very popular and was one of Cotton's biggest-selling records of the period. It also demonstrated how eager British bands were to emulate the style and success of their American heroes: Louis Armstrong had recorded 'Bessie' only eight months before, on 1 February 1930.

Despite Cotton's new wireless popularity and record hits, Ciro's management continued to insist that he keep his music at a low volume. This was something like standard West End procedure at the time; Lew Stone's band at the Monseigneur suffered the same fate soon afterwards. But Nat maintained that at times the music at Ciro's was so subdued the diners were audible as they delicately tucked into their caviar.

Ciro's also operated a sister-club of the same name in Paris, where the resident band was led by celebrated black bandleader Noble Sissle. The atmosphere at the French nightspot was more lively, however, and the patrons far more receptive to hot jazz. So, when management arranged for Billy Cotton to swap stands for a month with Sissle, both leader and sidemen were delighted. Not only could they let their hair down musically, they could also explore Paris and its nightlife – or whatever was left of it after work was over.

The exchange was enjoyable and successful for Cotton and crew, but when they arrived back in London Ciro's had seen a French revolution. Ignoring the management's forlorn pleas to keep the volume down, Noble Sissle and his players carried on blowing hot and strong. An all-black band in full, unrepentant flight sent the club's clientele into semi-hysteria. Applauding every hot tune with newfound enthusiasm, they invaded the dance floor – up to now reserved for decorous outings only – with wild abandon. Cotton and his band returned home to discover that Ciro's high-society clientele – including the Prince of Wales – were now crazy for jazz. 'When we came back from Paris,' Gonella told Sheila Tracy, 'this coloured band had been blowing their brains out and got away with murder and we got sacked straight away because we weren't as good as they were!' It was true: almost immediately Ciro's management decided to dispense with their British band and bring back Sissle. This decision led to at least one musical dividend for Cotton: trombonist Ellis Jackson defected from Sissle to join the British outcasts. A long-time Cotton stalwart, he played and danced with the band for decades thereafter.

Cotton rapidly dismissed the problem of his lost residency. Cashing in on radio popularity and growing record sales, he took his band out on a month's variety tour before taking a residency at Sherry's Ballroom, back in Brighton. As Summer 1931 approached, however, he faced a more serious setback: rheumatic fever, a life-threatening illness which jeopardised all his future activities. Sympathetic though his sidemen were, they also had to continue working; a long and indeterminate lay-off meant no money, so loyalties were constrained by necessity. It was at this time that Nat Gonella was approached on behalf of a star American bandleader. Roy Fox was in the process of recruiting a band to open a new club and restaurant in the heart of London's West End. 'Would Nat be interested?' The answer was an emphatic yes. Trumpeter Sid Buckman and trombonist Joe Ferrie similarly jumped at the chance.

When Cotton recovered he was furious to find that he had lost his entire brass section. 'Billy was a bit vindictive about that,' Gonella told Tracy, '– well, you couldn't blame him, losing [everyone] all at once.' In fact, Cotton may never have quite forgotten the matter. Thirty years on, Nat Gonella harboured this suspicion as an opportunity to appear on Cotton's *Band Show* – a peak-viewing Saturday-night television extravaganza – somehow never materialised. But Cotton gained a valuable trump card from their association: the policy of featuring a trumpeter-showman within his band ranks. In future years Teddy Foster, Jack Doyle and Grisha Farfel all filled the role and, later on, Bruts Gonella joined the Cotton brass section too, suggesting that even if such a grudge existed it wasn't extended to the rest of Nat's family.

Roy Fox remains one of the most famous names in British dance band history. Born in 1901 in Denver, Colorado, he sang with his local Salvation Army choir at three-years-old, took up the cornet at eleven, and following a brief spell as a bank messenger boy opted for a musical career. He subsequently progressed to the position of musical director for Hollywood's Fox Film Studios, then joined the renowned Abe Lyman Orchestra. With Lyman – like Henry 'Hotlips' Busse in Paul

Whiteman's orchestra – he developed the practice of playing softly into a megamute, earning the title of the 'Whispering Trumpet Player'. After a short stint with Lyman he left to form his own 'Montmartre Orchestra' and in 1929 came to London to form a band for an eight-week residency at the Café de Paris. Shortly after, he was appointed musical director for Decca Records and early in 1931 formed a new recording band whose cornermen included drummer Bill Harty, singer Al Bowlly and pianist/arranger Lew Stone. The band's new records were well received and Fox's American nationality was a distinct plus. Subsequently his name came to the attention of Jack Upson, a successful businessman, who was planning to open a new and exclusive nightclub, the Monseigneur, situated at No. 1 Piccadilly, in the heart of London's West End. Upson chose Fox to lead the band at the new club.

As the Monseigneur was to cater for high society, Fox thought it essential to assemble the best talent available, and this task he had entrusted to Bill Harty, a familiar figure in Archer Street and a shrewd operator. When Harty heard of Billy Cotton's unavoidable plight he moved fast as Fox's booking-agent to sign Gonella, Buckman and Ferrie; three emerging superstars of the dance band world, of whose talents he was already well aware. His hand-picked band would also include brothers Billy and Micky Amstell (altos) as well as Harry Berly (tenor) and Don Stuteley (double bass), though within a few months the Amstells had been replaced by Ernie Ritte and Jim Easton. Billy Amstell in due course became a celebrated cornerman of Ambrose's already well-established orchestra.

The opening of the Monseigneur in May 1931 was a sumptuous occasion. Packed with the cream of high society and boasting royal patronage from both the Prince of Wales and

Duke of Kent, the club was frequented by business and professional men of high influence, and wealthy Indian princes with their entourages. The restaurant itself, newly designed, dwarfed most of its West End opposition. Below ground level it boasted its own entrance in Piccadilly, a few yards from the Circus, and Lew Stone's widow, Joyce, later recalled that one visitor (a famous music publisher) was most impressed by the grandeur of the staircase:

> The walls were cloaked in maroon silk which matched a thick carpet. There was much gilded paintwork. At the foot of the stairs we were welcomed by a magnificent silver-bewigged flunkey, wearing a blue velvet suit with lace ruffles and closely resembling the portrait of 'The Monseigneur' that hung on the wall of the cocktail bar. There was a special Monseigneur cocktail. It was blue, based on gin and was naturally rattled in a cocktail shaker filled with ice cubes. It was popular so I assumed it was a pleasant appetiser!
>
> The ballroom was maroon, like the entrance, with huge gilt candlesticks on each side of the rostrum. Two sides of the room had a narrow upstairs balcony where one could eat without evening dress. A friend told me he used to consume bacon and eggs up there for the princely sum of ten shillings! There were gala evenings to celebrate the Derby, New Year's Eve and the Varsity Boat Race. The winning crew often dined there after a trip to the theatre. The dance floor was very small – possibly thirty feet by twenty feet. On really busy nights extra tables were added and the dance floor virtually ceased to exist. As well as the band there was the cabaret. Great artists appeared – Douglas Byng, Bea Lillie, Marion Harris and Lucienne Boyer (whose hit song was 'Parlez-moi d'amour').

Joyce was a regular visitor to the Monseigneur and as her relationship with Lew developed she was there more often. In 2004 – still youthful, wonderfully vivacious and travelling occasionally to the Lew Stone School of Music in Australia – she told Digby Fairweather:

> The Monseigneur had kitchens which served both the club and the grill room in Jermyn Street at the back. Sometimes when I was meeting Lew I would have come from a class [Stone is a classical pianist] and have music in my hand – maybe Bach – and would want to eat. Lew would say, 'I can't eat with you; I haven't got time.' And he would take me into the Monseigneur Grill where Tony Azenda was the head barman and Tony would put me at the bar and look after me.

The Monseigneur's management was possibly less demanding than Ciro's about the way the music was provided, but familiarity between musicians and patrons was discouraged. Requests, often accompanied by a five-pound note, were handed to Roy Fox on printed cards. Off the stand, band members were treated simply like other staff such as waiters or cooks. After they had completed a set and the relief band had taken over, Fox's musicians were dismissed to an ante-room to await their next stint, drink, eat and play cards. Such stern segregation between band and club visitors may have seemed strange to American bandleaders working in Britain; Fox himself, as well as Carroll Gibbons, Howard Jacobs, Jack Harris and Bert Ralton, would all have remembered a more easy-going atmosphere back home. At least one such leader was heard to remark of his uncommunicative onlookers, 'Look at them! You wouldn't think they were here to enjoy themselves!'

One Monseigneur patron, the Prince of Wales (later King Edward VIII), however, was always out for a good time. Observers noticed that the Prince and the young trumpet star in the section looked alike; both were short and fair-haired. And though conversation was forbidden, there was mutual acknowledgement; Nat via a half-bow from his seat in the trumpet section, the Prince by a wink over the shoulder of his dancing partner. One favourite of the royal visitor was 'Georgia on My Mind' and he would often send a note via a waiter to Roy Fox requesting the song. One evening Fox tried to substitute a different Gonella special, 'The Isle of Capri'. Later in the evening a second note arrived informing the bandleader that 'as much as he had enjoyed "The Isle of Capri",' His Royal Highness' preference was still for 'Georgia'.

Nat had played with Fox for less than two weeks when he received a rival offer from bandleader Bert Ambrose. Ambrose's incomparable orchestra held sway at the Mayfair Hotel and its leader was prepared to pay Gonella fifteen pounds a week, an extraordinarily high wage for the period and double his current earnings. As he had no contract with Fox, Nat handed in his notice and signed with the opposition. The American, however, was reluctant to lose his star sideman and agreed to match the offer. The tug of war that followed concluded with Nat's decision to remain with Fox (who had to pay compensation to his rival out of court); the trumpeter always remembered with a smile that he was the first dance band musician to have a transfer fee placed on his head.

During the early 1930s radio was the principal source of daily and nightly entertainment, and broadcasts by dance bands attracted huge listening figures. The BBC homed in on the Monseigneur after only a few months of the Fox residency and a contract was signed for half an hour's broadcast every Wednesday at 10.30 p.m. This was introduced by the plaintive sound of Fox's theme tune 'Whispering' featuring his muted trumpet and his follow-up announcement: 'Good evening ladies and gentlemen – this is Roy Fox speaking.' The orchestra also played stage shows at the Paramount Cinema, Regent Street, in between the movie screenings of the day.

In addition to this busy schedule, Fox's band recorded prolifically for Decca, including one of Nat's best-known song hits, 'Oh! Mo'nah', recorded on 30 December 1931. One earlier vocal, 'Tell Me, Are You from Georgia?', was shared with Al Bowlly on 18 August 1931. 'Oh! Mo'nah' (the title is a paraphrase of 'mourner' rather than a woman's name) was based on a southern spiritual, Nat taking the part of the preacher or 'caller' while the band became his answering congregation. The recorded result was – and remains – a catchy sing-along song in a (possibly anachronistic) country and western setting by Lew Stone. It would re-emerge as a significant Gonella hit some forty years later. One identifiable characteristic of his vocal style – an inability to pronounce the 'r' consonant – is first apparent on 'Oh! Mo'nah'; the phrase 'the lead horse sprung' emerges as 'spwung' and there are many other examples during the period and well after. However, many years later, in conversation, Nat did not appear to have the same problem.

At the Monseigneur, Gonella often found the on-stand discipline and need to suppress the volume restricting and regularly blew away the problem in late-night clubs. As he told Sheila Tracy:

> The main thing I used to do was go to the nightclubs and play jazz. Invariably it was the piano player who was in charge of the band and he'd say, 'We're going to play "Sweet Sue",' and I'd say I didn't know it and [he would reply], 'Well you will do by the second chorus,' and we learnt to listen with the ear. You got used to hearing chords and that was a great asset for playing jazz.
>
> The Nest was our number-one nightclub: marvellous place that was. In the Nest they'd be on the floor doing a shuffle-like dance and there'd be Armstrong, Cab Calloway or Duke Ellington and quite a few British bandleaders on the floor and I'd be playing trumpet. Some of these lads would come in a bit late, in evening

dress, having been on a society gig, and they'd go down to the end of the ballroom, put two tables there, and go back the other end and run and dive over the two tables. The Nest was what they called a bottle party, which meant you bought a bottle and had to have it stored.

It was after one such session, a little later in the band's career at the Monseigneur, that Gonella introduced Al Bowlly to the woman who would become his first wife. As dawn was breaking the trumpeter would head for Lyons' Corner House in Piccadilly for breakfast. Until well after the war the West End's Corner Houses were unofficial meeting places for night people – musicians, entertainers, nightclub staff and prostitutes among them. On one such early morning Bowlly joined Nat for a fried breakfast, and while they were sipping tea Freda Roberts, known to Nat as a hostess from the Bag o' Nails, came across to join their table. He introduced her to Bowlly. It was plain that sexual chemistry was exploding but as the singer was dark, handsome and a celebrity – as well as a lady's man – it seemed likely that this would be no more than a casual affair. It came as a shock both to Nat and other members of the band, many of whom knew Freda, when shortly afterwards she and Bowlly married. The union lasted for only a few weeks, however, as – while Freda had explained to Bowlly that she intended to keep her friends after marriage – she had omitted to mention that menfriends were included in the policy.

After six months, a dramatic development threatened the Monseigneur's great house band when Roy Fox contracted pleurisy. After attempting to continue for a short time, he handed his baton over to Lew Stone while, on doctors' orders, he went to Switzerland to recover his strength in a small village high in the Alps.

Stone was a popular choice. Known to his fellow sidemen as

'Mr Nice Guy', he was a superb arranger and talented pianist whose work had done much to establish Fox's high musical reputation. While Fox recuperated, his orchestra maintained its non-stop radio and recording schedule (under its absent leader's name), all the time gaining in popularity. Nat Gonella's first recording of his soon-to-be theme song, Hoagy Carmichael's 'Georgia on My Mind' was cut for Decca on 4 February 1932 with Lew Stone in command.

Naturally, listeners thought that 'Georgia' was dedicated to the American state, but another theory is that the song was inspired by a girlfriend of Carmichael's sister. Richard Sudhalter's biography of Hoagy, *Stardust Melody*, noted that 'perhaps intentionally the lyric is ambiguous; is the Georgia of the singer's thoughts and longings simply a place or is the apostrophe also to a person?' In any case, Carmichael's songs – among them 'Stardust', 'Rockin' Chair', 'Lazy River' (with Sidney Arodin), 'Moon Country' and 'Down t'Uncle Bill's' – would remain regular vehicles for Gonella down the decades.

His first recording of 'Georgia' was not, however, to everyone's liking. One Decca director wrote to Lew Stone: 'I think you have spoiled an excellent record by the appalling vocal refrain. If you put out any more records like this, the public will soon switch their interests elsewhere.' This was quickly disproved. 'Georgia' became a high seller, which helped to revive the flagging fortunes of E. R. Lewis' Decca company, and the song would remain associated with Gonella for life. 'A day without having to sing it,' he once told Ron Brown, 'is like Christmas.'

While Fox was away, his line-up remained largely unchanged, but one major acquisition was the replacement of Don Stuteley by the diminutive, dynamic Tiny Winters, a premier exponent of slap-bass. Born in Hackney in 1908, Winters –

who had earlier played briefly with Ambrose's orchestra – had been inspired to take up the bass by Britain's Spike Hughes, and American 'Pops' Foster's work on Luis Russell's 'Jersey Lightning' had opened a door for the young musician. Fellow East Enders, Winters and Gonella formed an affectionate friendship, terminated only by the bassist's death in 1996.

Meanwhile, Roy Fox's health continued to improve until, after five months, medical advisers decided that he was well enough to come back to London and resume bandleading. He had stayed in touch with Stone, telephoning from his retreat after each Wednesday-night broadcast, and on his arrival home was quick to realise that his band had improved tremendously under Stone's guiding hand and was now rivalling Ambrose's superb unit for top dance band honours in Britain. Nevertheless, Fox was reluctant to stay in nightclubs and wanted stage-fame too; just before his Swiss sojourn his orchestra had appeared for a week on-stage at the Carlton Cinema in London's Haymarket. The pressures of such doubling had prompted the presence of Fox's doctor in his dressing room, but the orchestra had made a hit, which prompted Fox, on his return, to embark on more stage dates, this time at the London Palladium.

At first, the Monseigneur management was happy to agree to Fox's concerts as long as his band was back on-stage at the club by 9.30 for evening sessions. Unfortunately, they were sometimes delayed by half an hour or more, placing extra burdens on the supporting band, Mantovani and his Salon Orchestra.

Eventually the management complained to Fox, but he wanted to emulate the success of bandleaders like Jack Hylton, and was reluctant to refuse prestigious stage appearances. In consequence the dissatisfied employers approached Lew

Stone with an offer: would he take over the band on a permanent basis? Stone agreed and the management duly gathered the musicians together to explain the position. They could either leave with Fox or remain at the Monseigneur with Stone as their new leader. Such a takeover naturally created controversy and versions of the story vary with the teller. In 2004, Joyce Stone, Lew's widow, remembered:

> I was dancing at the Monseigneur one evening with a young nephew of Jack Upson (who was not only the owner of the club but also, of course, of the Dolcis shoe company). Well, as we danced around the floor my partner asked Roy for a request and he turned it down – rather rudely. When we'd danced around the floor again the request was repeated – and turned down again quite brusquely! Obviously Roy had no idea of whom he was talking to, but I suspect the story got back!

Fox himself (in his autobiography *Hollywood, Mayfair and All That Jazz*) portrayed the takeover differently:

> About this time my contract at the club was about to be renewed, but when it came to discussing it with the owner it transpired we couldn't agree on terms. I thought the band had earned more money through its popularity but he didn't seem to think so. The outcome was I decided to leave. I told the boy... and of course they were surprised. A couple of nights later they all asked me to meet them there after work and told me that Lew Stone had been approached – and inasmuch as they didn't know where I would be going with the band, they decided to remain. I'm sure the boys thought if I lost the Monseigneur I was finished. Well, it didn't turn out that way at all.

With trumpeter/vocalist Sid Buckman as his only remaining sideman, Fox formed an all-new band, opening one night later at the Café Anglais, Leicester Square, and later the Kit Kat Club to more success.

Nat Gonella was sorry to say goodbye to Buckman, a regular colleague since the Billy Cotton band, but Stone engaged a fine replacement: trumpeter Alfie Noakes, who joined from Sidney Kyte's orchestra at the Piccadilly Hotel. And the general mood of the band was highly optimistic and much in favour of the new situation. Their new leader was popular and a skilled musician who set out to exploit all the talents of his jazz-friendly cornermen.

New additions to his band included Lew Davis (one of Britain's greatest pre-war trombonists), the equally formidable Joe Crossman (alto), and Eddie Carroll (piano). With Stone now directing, the band's full line-up comprised: Gonella and Noakes (trumpets); Joe Ferrie and Davis (trombone); Harry Berly, Crossman, Ernie Ritte, and Jim Easton (saxophones); Carroll (piano); Tiny Winters (bass); Bill Harty (drums) and singer/guitarist Al Bowlly. A formidable all-star aggregation. Together, they continued to play night by night to full houses at the Monseigneur.

Joyce Stone told the story of her first meetings with Gonella at this time to Digby Fairweather in 2004:

> When did I first meet Nat to talk to? Probably at one of those 'caffs' where they used to go during the interval when they were doing shows such as Lewisham Hippodrome. Also at one point Lew did two weeks at the Hammersmith Palais and I remember getting a friend to take me there – that was before Lew and I were married, just seeing each other occasionally – and I think Nat was there then. What was he like as a man? Well, rough, down to earth, polite in his own way, never rude, respectful to me, always himself – never put on airs and graces. One other member of the group, for example, who had the same background, acquired an Oxford accent nevertheless – not Nat! You knew exactly where you were with him. And as a performer of course – well, he was good, wasn't he? *The trumpet player!* Who else at that time could do

what he did? – the best lead, the best jazzman and a fantastic solo star.

In addition to his studio work with Stone's band, Nat's independent recording career proceeded apace. On 14 September 1932, with Harry Jacobson (piano/celeste), Al Bowlly (guitar), Tiny Winters (bass) and Bill Harty (drums), he made his first solo records – 'I Can't Believe that You're in Love with Me' and 'I Heard' – billed as 'Nat Gonella and His Trumpet'. These were followed on 15 November by 'Rockin' Chair' and 'When You're Smiling' and, on 3 March 1933, by 'Sing (It's Good for You)' and 'That's My Home'. Six more titles – 'Georgia on My Mind', 'Sweet Sue' (issued originally as by the 'Belgian Olympia Orchestra with Hot Trumpet'), 'Moon Country', 'Troublesome Trumpet', 'Carolina' and 'I Can't Dance, I Got Ants in My Pants' – followed with an enlarged group. Then, in November 1934, the first titles were recorded by 'Nat Gonella and his Georgians'.

In the same period Nat also recorded with Edgar Jackson's Dance Orchestra, Ray Starita's Ambassadors, Ray Noble and Sam Browne and the Blue Mountaineers, sharing vocals with Browne on numbers including 'Fit as a Fiddle', 'Sweet Sixteen and Never Been Kissed', 'You've Got Me Crying Again' and 'Cabin in the Pines'.

In 1932 Decca also re-released on their Mayfair label several of Gonella's early titles, credited to 'Eddie Hines and His Trumpet'. Record executives apparently decided that 'Eddie Hines' looked more impressive on a record label. (They may also have thought, of course, that two apparently different trumpet soloists might sell more records than one.) Nat's sides, re-released as by Eddie Hines, comprised his first two titles plus 'Rockin' Chair' and 'When You're Smiling'.

The first few years of the 1930s had proved busy and exciting times for the Cockney trumpeter, still only in his mid-twenties. His star was destined to shine more brightly as the decade rolled on.

4

Get Hot*

Louis Armstrong was the central musical influence in Nat Gonella's musical career. The two men became lifelong friends; letters and telegrams passed between them from the time of their first meeting and Nat would proudly attest that, on arrival in Britain, Armstrong's opening enquiries would regularly include 'How's my boy Nat?' The first of their meetings was in July 1932.

That month, Armstrong arrived in Britain for a two-week booking at the London Palladium followed by a tour of Britain's number-one variety theatres. *Dance Band News* – like every other music trade paper of the day – headlined the event: 'Coloured trumpet king to appear at Palladium'. Nat and Bruts Gonella were determined to absorb every note, every trick, every stage device of their hero. They booked front-row seats for his opening night, then seats for the whole of the first week (twice nightly) and 'rover' tickets for the sec-

*Parlophone, Nat Gonella and his Georgians, 28.5.36

ond week, which allowed them to sit in any part of the auditorium. Throughout, they remained mesmerised by Armstrong.

Other musicians were in the audience too, but a few – like some members of the public – initially found his presence bizarre and his music overpowering. 'The business for Armstrong's first visit to the Palladium,' Gonella told critic Max Jones and John Chilton later (for their 1971 biography *Louis*), 'was said to be a record for the theatre at that time. So that every performance would be full at Louis' opening but by the time he had to finish, the theatre was half empty!' The superstar and his elemental trumpet constituted medicine too potent for visitors used to more sedate entertainment. 'The sweating, strutting figure in the spotlight hitting endless high notes,' critic Iain Lang commented in retrospect, 'had only a tenuous and intermittent connection with the creator of the intensely moving music of "West End Blues" and "Muggles".' Some deserters would vacate their seats and creep down the aisle towards the exit sign while the house lights were dimmed and Nat and Bruts, sitting on the floor with their rover tickets looking down the aisle at the stage, would regularly trip them up in the darkness. 'I don't think Armstrong was too upset about the people who left,' Nat told Digby Fairweather. 'I think he sort of swallowed it, you know. I think he could understand people's feelings – that they didn't quite know it.'

Nat was in the informal work-centre for London musicians, Archer Street – which he always described as the 'street of good hope' – when the word was passed around that Armstrong was staying at a small hotel in the Strand. 'They wouldn't have coloured people in the big hotels,' Gonella told Sheila Tracy. 'I think Duke Ellington was the first one they allowed in to the Dorchester.' Not only that, but Armstrong's instrument was being cleaned and serviced in Boosey and

Hawkes' music shop nearby. Nat was friendly with the store's manager, and called on him for a private viewing of the visitor's B-flat trumpet.

'When is it going back?' he asked.

'About ten minutes' time,' came the reply, and after a short negotiation Nat set off for the Strand, Armstrong's trumpet under one arm. On arrival at the hotel, having bartered his way past the doorman, he came face to face with Armstrong's unpopular manager Johnny Collins, but refused to accept the instruction to 'leave Louis' trumpet with me'. 'It's got to be a personal delivery,' he insisted, and finally Collins gave him Armstrong's room number. The door opened to reveal Louis himself, just out of bed in mid-afternoon, and Gonella could hardly believe his eyes. Quickly the two men fell into a two-hour conversation, during which Armstrong took a liking to his brash young visitor. 'I spent most of the time telling him how good *I* was!' Nat told Digby Fairweather later. He was quick to follow up the point to Armstrong that a good deal of the groundwork for his success had been laid by British imitators such as Gonella himself. The visiting star, genial as always, accepted the point with a laugh. But he also received a favour from his visitor. One of his suitcases had been mislaid in transit and Armstrong had only one suit at the hotel. Nat found an iron and pressed his host's suit for him prior to a press interview, a favour which, characteristically, Louis remembered and repeated to reporters when he toured Britain in later years. 'I think seeing him that first time after carrying his trumpet around was probably the greatest moment of my life,' Gonella told Sheila Tracy. 'I couldn't believe it because he was like a god.'

Apart from their bond of jazz the two men found that their lives had run on uncannily similar lines. Louis had been born in Jane Alley, New Orleans, in a tough area of the city known as 'the battlefield'; Nat in Battle Bridge, a similarly tough area of north London. Armstrong had been raised in a waifs' home, where he was introduced to music by a qualified teacher, Joseph Jones; Nat in a guardian school where William Clarke occupied a parallel post. And both had had personal idols: Armstrong revered his former leader Joe 'King' Oliver, while Nat, of course, revered Armstrong himself. There was even a visual resemblance between the short, stocky, oval-faced men. Such coincidences occurred to Digby Fairweather too, when he visited Gonella in 1984. Fairweather noted later:

> As we sat in his neat Gosport sitting room, surrounded by reminders of days now long gone, my eyes were attracted to one particular photograph, a dark rotogravure of a young Louis Armstrong, wing-collared with handsome face turned halfway to the camera and trumpet held proudly. 'What a wonderful picture of Louis,' I said. 'Look again,' responded Nat. 'It's me!' I looked again and thought about the profound coincidence of two men born before the advent of either radio or television a thousand miles apart. The shared youth: in poverty, then in a board school. The mutual urge to play the trumpet; the shared and strangely complementary careers, records played by chance in a shop and – perhaps the most unlikely gift of fate – a trumpet left in a London music store for repair. I looked once more at the short, still stocky man before me with his cheery face, cratered lips and pert quick sparrow's movements. 'Did you ever think that there might be something a bit more than coincidence about it all?' The head cocked for a moment to consider, then smiled across. 'Yes I did,' he said quickly and finally.

The origin of Armstrong's nickname 'Satchmo' is now famously accredited to Percy Mathison Brooks, one-time editor of the *Melody Maker*, Britain's most influential music weekly of the twentieth century. What is less widely acknowledged is that – as Armstrong explained during a 1956 interview for the *Daily Mail* – Nat Gonella was the agent for its invention. In 1932 he had introduced Brooks to his new friend with the words 'Meet Louis Satchelmouth Armstrong!' Brooks responded with an anglicised abbreviation: 'Well, hello – Satchmo!' And the abbreviation stuck.

Just as Nat attended every concert of Armstrong's, Louis reciprocated by going to hear Gonella whenever his schedule allowed (including at the London Palladium); potentially, this was an intimidating situation for any trumpeter who lacked Gonella's cocksure confidence and vigour. One night Armstrong and his entourage, including manager Johnny Collins, visited the Monseigneur and Collins – free from the prohibition laws of America – drank until he passed out, head down on the club table. At this point, a journalist who had joined the party asked Armstrong a familiar question of the time: what tune did he enjoy playing most of all? Casting a disgusted gaze towards his inert manager, the trumpeter growled, 'I'll Be Glad When You're Dead, You Rascal You!'

After his Palladium fortnight Armstrong embarked on a variety tour. Pianist/arranger Billy Mason's Hot Rhythm Recording Band (including Bruts Gonella and Harry Hayes) backed Louis and also on the bill were British comedy stars including Tommy Handley, Ted Ray, Ethel Revnell, Gracie West, dancers and acrobats.

Louis and Nat met as often as possible while Armstrong was in London, usually finishing the night at a late club when performances were over. The Bag o' Nails in Kingly Street, the Nest in Little Pulteney Street (now Brewer Street), and the 43 Club were all popular late venues for bottle parties and jam sessions. But Louis favoured Jig's Club (124–126 Wardour Street) run by Alec and Rose Ward, which catered largely for

West Indians. Jig's (the word was black slang for 'negro') served red beans and rice (Armstrong's favourite meal) and hosted early-morning jam sessions. On one occasion a whole troupe of black dancing girls from the London Coliseum arrived there. Amid much hilarity they taught Nat and Louis to dance the 'Shimmy', swaying in between the club tables.

Gonella was by now living in the heart of the West End (and round the corner from the Monseigneur) on the third floor of 116 Shaftesbury Avenue. Armstrong regularly joined him there to chat, exchange trumpet talk, play and drink. 'He didn't actually stay at the flat,' Gonella told Fairweather, 'but he'd visit. He'd come up Sunday night when he wasn't working. We'd maybe put the radio on, and he'd scat to some of the hymns and that. We were up on the third floor and we could see Piccadilly Circus out of our window. He'd smoke muggles [marijuana] all the time. And we'd always have some beer for him.' The picture is an irresistible one. Sometimes Nat would ask musical questions and Armstrong would demonstrate the answer; a master-class of incomparable value.

In 2004 Albert Torrance told Fairweather a revealing story about Armstrong and his relationship with his British friend. 'You know about some of the silly things that get said from time to time. I went on a one-night stand with Louis and inevitably the conversation started; somebody started trying to tell Louis that Nat was just copying him! Louis Armstrong would not have that under any circumstances. He said, "That's absolutely wrong! That boy can really play the trumpet. And he's got his own ideas." In my opinion,' Torrance concluded, 'Armstrong was a really nice bloke.'

Throughout their 1930s friendship, Armstrong frequently called on Nat to act as unofficial greeter for black Americans visiting Britain. On Louis' instructions, Cab Calloway, Fats

Waller and the original Mills Brothers called Gonella on arrival in London and he would help them find what they needed.

Throughout 1932–33, the Lew Stone Orchestra rapidly turned into a premier national attraction. Its new leader was stretching his own and his players' talents to their limits and he maintained a constantly high reputation among his sidemen as both a gentleman and a popular leader. Stone – an efficient classical pianist – had been introduced to hot music by listening to Percy Cowell's five-piece band at London's Strand Corner House. Later he turned professional through the good offices of Len Daniels, brother of celebrated drummer Joe Daniels, and became staff arranger for Ambrose's great orchestra After taking over Fox's orchestra he deliberately adopted a broad policy and, as he remembered later:

> The first question in forming a band was – who did I want to play to? [Then] I started thinking about the different phases that people go through – as youngsters looking for excitement – in their twenties falling in love – getting older, gathering more experience. Listening to our Tuesday-night radio show people got used to the fact that if there was something they disliked it wouldn't last more than three minutes. Either side of the more outlandish things – say 'Call of the Freaks' – I would have maybe a warm sentimental number sung by Al Bowlly. [But] if I didn't think Al Bowlly was right for a given song I would use the musician that could interpret it better.*

Thus, although Al Bowlly remained the principal star, additional support was provided by a team of musician/singers (known within the band as the 'Lew-groaners'): Joe Crossman, Jim Easton, Nat, and Tiny Winters, whose high-pitched voice

* Quoted from CD insert for *A Tribute to Lew Stone*.

was ideal for female hit tunes including, among others, Ella Fitzgerald's 'Sing Me a Swing Song (and Let Me Dance)' and, occasionally to Winters' slight chagrin, 'Oh you nasty man!' As a result, he was startled and amused to receive fan mail regularly addressed to 'Miss' and, from France on one occasion, 'Mademoiselle' Tiny Winters.

Stone was always on the lookout for new ideas, including comedy material, and possibly his most successful invention was 'Little Nell', a musical spoof-drama which caused such a sensation when first broadcast that it was repeated for weeks thereafter. High-voiced Winters played Nell, Jim Easton her father, Al Bowlly the villain and Nat Gonella the 'constabule'. 'It was a dark and stormy night when my Nellie went away,' the routine began, and finished with the promise: 'And all next week we play East Lynn!'

The Stone band was by now a musical sensation too. The liner notes to *A Tribute to Lew Stone* provide Stone's explanation: 'What I went out for was to get a band of ten musicians that sounded like ten fingers at a piano. So that it played as one person! It wasn't a pick-up band – it was a team. The individuals within the band were brought out during our playing.' The philosophy recalls that of Duke Ellington, and it is regrettable that – even in the twenty-first century – pre-war British dance bands still tend to be confined in critical perceptions to a drab cultural backwater of their own, whereas their American counterparts are far more properly and realistically assessed. Stone's band (like Ray Noble's at the period) compares more than favourably with many American contemporaries, and his output was not only more jazz-based than that of most of his fellow leaders in Britain but (almost invariably) innovatory, musical and above all appealingly listenable. In 2005 the recordings still sound as fresh, brash and creative as they did then. One can still imagine Stone fans, seventy years ago, crowded around their wireless sets once a week – or perhaps rolling back the carpet to dance – as the band made its regular broadcast, from the Monseigneur, ten-thirty to midnight, Tuesday night.

In the early months of 1933 the BBC acquired its first competitor in the form of commercial radio. The Palmolive Soap Company, prominent as a sponsor on American radio, signed its first long-term contracts to sponsor broadcasts to Britain from the Continent. But it was the Bush Radio Company that sponsored the first programmes featuring complete shows with live artists rather than gramophone records. Most of Britain's top bands could be heard on Radio Luxembourg, Radio Normandy and Radio Lyons; the programmes were usually recorded in a London studio, and cut onto fragile discs, which made transportation a matter of extreme care, especially where 'soap' radio serials were concerned.

On 26 May 1933 Nat Gonella cut a record with the gifted black pianist/entertainer Garland Wilson. Originally from Martinsburg, West Virginia, where he was born in 1909, Wilson made his name in New York as accompanist for Nina Mae McKinney and came to Europe with her in 1932. From 1933 he played long residencies in both Paris and London, recording with both Gonella and Jack Payne. The trumpeter had good reason to remember the date with Wilson as it was one of the quickest records he ever made. A recording studio had been booked from nine in the morning until one o'clock, but at eleven there was still no sign of the American visitor and a search ensued. Eventually he was traced to a hotel room, still in bed and asleep, and a taxi was called. On arrival, the two men had fifteen minutes left to record their two sides and, with no time to rehearse, cut straight into 'Nobody's

Sweetheart' (a galloping carefree performance) and 'Stormy Weather'. The record is marvellous, but Gonella was glad to be out of the studio as Wilson – a gay cabaret performer – took a fancy to the trumpeter, making it apparent with winks, smiles and a friendly arm around his new colleague.

In summer 1933 the Monseigneur closed for six weeks, leaving Lew Stone's orchestra temporarily out of work. So, when Ray Noble (whose British session recordings of the period are of international standard) was invited to take a band to Holland for a four-week engagement, many of Stone's players, who had recorded with Noble, were glad to go. They included Tiny Winters, Al Bowlly and Alfie Noakes, and although Nat Gonella was initially reluctant to fly – this was in aviation's early years – eventually he was persuaded. With some trepidation the Noble ensemble boarded their charter plane and after a safe landing at Rotterdam Airport posed with relief for a publicity shot in front of their aircraft.

Their trip was a continual round of music and pleasure and it laid the foundations – for Nat Gonella – of a friendship with Dutch jazz lovers intermittently spanning forty years. The destination was Scheveningen, a fashionable Dutch seaside resort. The venue for their short season was its Kurhaus, an impressive leisure complex graced with a large terrace for tea-dances in fine weather. Fortunately the sun shone brilliantly through the entire four weeks, so such dances were a daily occurrence before the band moved indoors to play in the magnificent ballroom. The atmosphere, more free and easy than at the Monseigneur, meant that the band enjoyed themselves as much as the dancers did. And whenever Al Bowlly took the microphone Dutch women crowded closer to the bandstand, just as Americans would for Frank Sinatra ten years later. Bowlly was accompanied on the trip by his second wife Marjie and was formally referred to in the Dutch press as Albert A. Bowlly.

Off the stand, the Noble band members were treated like royalty and were regularly offered champagne and strawberries. (Winters remembered that several sidemen, no doubt hung-over, asked for a good British cup of tea instead!) And, taking advantage of the glorious weather, the ensemble, on free days, made the most of the beaches. Bowlly (a keep-fit enthusiast), Gonella and Winters often entertained friends with comedy gymnastics on the beach, some of which were filmed on Winters' home-movie camera. The movies and photographs of the trip show male members of the party decked out in vests as well as trunks, and Nat Gonella in a black skull-cap which struck Ron Brown as making him look like Emperor Ming from *The Adventures of Flash Gordon*. The Noble ensemble also filmed a cinema 'short' during their stay and a copy exists in the archives of collector-producer Dave Bennett.

Through radio broadcasts and records, most of the visiting Britons were well-known in Holland and their Dutch hosts extended them warm welcomes at every turn. 'One local,' Tiny Winters recalled, 'said, "Come! I have a houseboat. It is beautiful – and you can sleep in it." When we got there it turned out he meant a boat-house!' Freddy Gardner, his wife, Winters and Gonella were similarly chagrined by the cost of a taxi both ways as well as the hire of a boatman to ferry them to their hosts. Other offers, however, were more fruitful, and after four weeks of celebration – and an average of four hours of sleep a night – Nat Gonella was shattered by the time he said goodbye to his new Dutch friends. He was last to board the plane home and found that the only seat available was an ordinary chair, on which he was required to perch for the whole flight.

Back in Britain he booked into a nursing home for recuperative purposes, a dignified predecessor to what is now known (presumably) as 'rehab'.

By mid-September, however, Gonella had recovered sufficiently to begin the Monseigneur's autumn season with his colleagues. Recording sessions were also resumed, and scarcely a week passed without a new Lew Stone record arriving in the shops. Nat lent his trumpet talents to jazz-filled titles such as 'Blue Prelude', 'Blue Jazz', 'White Jazz', 'Tiger Rag', 'Canadian Capers' and 'Milenberg Joys'. As Stone's band's reputation continued to grow, rival bandleaders, including Jack Hylton, regularly made offers for his sidemen and stars while Henry Hall, leader of the BBC Dance Orchestra, tried to lure away the entire brass section. Its members thought the offer over seriously until the Monseigneur's management offered them more money and loyalty to their well-liked leader prevailed.

Although the volume of fan mail the band received in the wake of broadcasts and records was highly flattering, the Stone ensemble realised the full extent of their popularity only when Lew took them on tour during a break from the Monseigneur residency. At major venues in cities around the country, fans turned out in their thousands to see the band, resulting in crowd scenes that were actually frightening. Many such fans were women who had come to hear – and perhaps to catch an off-stage glimpse of – Al Bowlly. One concert that Nat would never forget took place at the Birmingham Palais de Dance. Two thousand people paid five shillings each to jam-pack the venue, making dancing an impossibility.

Such ecstatic receptions gave Gonella the beginnings of an idea. Bowlly might be the bigger star, but whenever Nat himself took front-of-stage to play or sing there was a comparable reaction. One day, therefore, why should he not be on-stage fronting his own band?

During the summer of 1934, the opportunity arose. Stone's band played short residencies at the Café Anglais and the Hollywood Restaurant in Piccadilly. At the Hollywood, Gonella and Stone had a minor disagreement and subsequently agreed to part company, a dramatic decision which, nevertheless, did not bother Nat overmuch. He settled a date to appear at the Grafton Rooms, Liverpool, on the night that King George V and Queen Mary were due to open the newly completed Mersey Tunnel, and Liverpool's nightlife should be booming. In the event, however, the city was ablaze with other attractions: street bands, illuminated tramcars, firework displays and much else in the way of free entertainment. When Nat took the stand for his solo debut there were sixteen people in the audience and the percentage revenue did not even cover his travelling expenses.

Riding the setback, he carried on recording as a soloist for Decca and undertaking promotional appearances, often in big department stores. One such date was at the Bon Marche in Brixton, where violinist Brian Lawrance and his Quaglino Quartette – Frank Gregori (accordion), Harold Hood (piano), Mark Sheridan (guitar) and Harry Wilson (bass) – were already playing. They backed Nat for several tunes and the combination worked so well that the band decided to approach impresario George Black for an audition. Black liked what he heard and booked them for a tour, opening at the Holborn Empire, one of London's most legendary variety theatres. This was to be the first time Nat saw his name in large letters over a theatre, topping the bill as 'England's reply to America's hottest', and the week that followed was a triumph, culminating in two encores on closing night. The front page of *Melody Maker* for

30 June 1934 was headlined 'Gonella Sauce Makes New Rhythm Dish Appetizing!' and went on to note, 'The stylish Lawrance contrasts well with the Cagney-like impudence of the fair-haired Gonella.' Praise was also heaped on pianist Harold Hood as a 'brilliant young swing pianist'. Less than a year later Hood – known as 'Babe' – would join Nat in his Georgians. And among support acts at the Empire there appeared Dick Henderson – a short rotund man in a bowler hat who danced 'Tiptoe Through the Tulips' to the tinkling carillon of hundreds of bells hidden in his pockets and strapped to his legs.

The same edition of the *Melody Maker* also reported that Louis Armstrong had completed the final week of his 1934 British tour at the Grand Theatre, Derby, and was leaving for the USA. On arrival home, the piece noted, Armstrong would be without a manager. He had finally broken free from Johnny Collins.

While Nat was enjoying his new solo success, Lew Stone made a re-appearance in his star trumpeter's dressing room. Differences were resolved and Nat agreed to return to the Stone band as soon as his commitments with Brian Lawrance were completed. In the interim, Bruts Gonella took his brother's place with Stone for an Isle of Man residency but – for their last date – Stone was keen for Gonella to appear in person. So it was arranged that immediately after he had played his final note at Finsbury Park Empire the trumpeter would set off for the Isle of Man. Accordingly he drove to Blackpool, arriving there at seven in the morning in order to fly by light aircraft to his destination by lunchtime, and thereafter catch some sleep. Persuasion from Stone's musicians led him on to the golf course instead, and once the concert was over band members packed immediately and rushed to catch the night-boat back to the mainland. Gonella collected his car from Blackpool to motor directly to London. He made it safely but, 'Boy, was I tired,' he said.

Thereafter for a short spell Nat doubled engagements with Lew Stone and Brian Lawrance, but it was a strain and after one more successful week at the Palladium, he decided to give up the partnership with Lawrance. This proved to be a wise move as it was indirectly to prompt the creation of 'Nat Gonella's Georgians' mark 1 – as a band-within-a-band for Lew Stone. Their first appearance was at the Leeds Empire, where Gonella – with Don Barrigo (tenor), Eddie Carroll (piano) and Tiny Winters (bass), augmented by an outsider, Nat's former bandleader Bob Dryden (drums) – finished the first half of Stone's show.

By now, Stone's orchestra featured singer Alan Kane and drummer Jock Jacobsen in place of Al Bowlly and Bill Harty. The two absentees had accompanied Ray Noble to America, where his British recordings were (rightly) revered; Harty was his business manager and Bowlly, of course, his star vocalist. Their departure was a blow to Stone, but he weathered the problem in his normal kindly fashion and, as usual, made no attempt to block his colleagues' career-move.

By late 1934 the Monseigneur's winter season was in full swing and members of the Stone aggregation were closing the first half of a variety show at the Finsbury Park Empire before hastening south to the West End for their club commitment. Gonella, however, had his eye on the future. 'An ambitious young musician is not the most loyal person to have in a band,' he admitted later, and his dream – as he raced between venues – was now, quite definitely, to front a band of his own. Plans were already being laid.

On 2 November that year the first records announcing the

existence of Nat Gonella and his Georgians – including 'Don't Let Your Love Go Wrong', 'Moonglow' and 'Foxtrot Medley, Part 1' ('Troublesome Trumpet', 'Dinah', 'Let Him Live') and 'Part 2' ('Oh! Mo'nah', 'Georgia on My Mind' and 'Sing – It's Good for You') – were cut for Parlophone, with a group comprising Albert Torrance (alto), Don Barrigo and George Evans (tenors), Harold Hood (piano), Arthur Baker (guitar), Will Hemmings (bass) and Bob Dryden (drums). And throughout the first three months of 1935 Nat returned to the studios to record a further twelve titles under the same banner with a variety of musicians including Bruts Gonella, Johnny Morrison, Ernest Ritte, tenorist Pat Smuts and guitarist/singer Jimmy Messini, as well as the celebrated pianist Monia Liter.

During this period Nat came to realise that certain of his recording colleagues were working with him only in the hope of finding favour with Stone, a secondary consideration which spurred him on further to find loyal partners for a band of his own. At last the decision was made and – for the final time – Gonella handed in his notice to Lew Stone.

5

*Music Maestro Please!**

Gonella's departure from Stone was both amicable and without regret, despite the fact that by this time he was earning a (then phenomenal) forty-five pounds a week. As a bandleader, he was well aware that he could command fees well beyond even such handsome wages. Joyce Stone remembers: 'Lew and Nat talked about it, and their relationship remained excellent. Nat became very keen to get his own group and Lew encouraged his solo career. If any of Lew's musicians wanted to find their own sextet, or whatever it was, Lew would say, "Well, I'll help you!" Lew made a lot of musicians into what they became later and if a player had a spark of talent Lew would encourage it – because he knew he could find someone else to take his place!'

Stone's replacement was the Scottish trumpeter Thomas Mossie McQuater, born in Maybole, Ayrshire, in September 1914 and six and a half years Gonella's junior. Tommy McQuater – who had quickly outgrown one early teacher and

*Parlophone, Nat Gonella and his Georgians, 5.10.38

polished up his cornet playing in a hometown brass band – would later build a legendary career as both jazz and lead trumpeter with, among others, Ambrose, the Squadronaires, the Skyrockets, Kenny Baker's Dozen and Jack Parnell's ATV Orchestra. In 2004 he was still playing at the Ealing Jazz Festival. That year he told Digby Fairweather about his 1935 career-move and how he first met Nat Gonella:

> I was working with Jack Payne at the time, in variety and at a Piccadilly club. We just generally said hello, talked about trumpets and things – and Louis Armstrong! I'd seen Louis in Glasgow – gave him a wave across the street – and Paris, various places, but I was always working when he was in London. But I thought Nat was great. A rough and ready working-class lad, like myself. And we got on well; used to meet down Archer Street later, after he had his Georgians. He had a lot of great qualities – even his singing – and he was a strong player, a great jazzman and lead in Lew's band, which he split with Alfie Noakes as I did later.
>
> How did I come to replace him? Well, I got a phone call from Lew Stone; he called me and said, 'I'd like you to do an audition.' I said, 'An audition? Oh well, all right then!' So it was arranged. I'm talking away [with members of the band listening]. 'An audition?' 'Yes.' 'Saturday morning?' 'Yes! At the Monseigneur in Piccadilly'... Anyhow, everything was arranged and then all of a sudden I got a call from Jack Payne that he had called a rehearsal for the same day I was doing the audition. Now, we never used to rehearse – it was always on the job. So he did it – well – out of spite really. So I rang Lew and I said, 'I'm afraid I can't do it! Jack Payne's called a rehearsal and I've got to do it by contract.' He [agreed a new time and] said, 'OK! This time we'll do it – but don't tell anyone. Not even your best friend.' So I went and did the audition and then off to France with Payne for the last job.
>
> At that time Nat lived in Shaftesbury Avenue, above the optician where I went, and I had to meet him there to get his grey band-suit. It more or less fitted – so it was just sent to the clean-

ers! But Lew Stone was good to me. He didn't ask me to take over Nat's features – I just used to play the jazz things and I did my own thing with 'St Louis Blues'.

Now, for Nat, the break had been made. On 1 April 1935 – a potentially ironic date – his band was due to open at the Newcastle Empire as 'Nat Gonella and his Georgians – Britain's Hottest Quintette' with two shows at 6.30 and 8.45. This was to be the first of a series of dates in a variety tour in which Nat co-topped the bill with comedians Naughton and Gold (fugitives from the 'Crazy Gang') above a supporting cast including Elsie Prince, Betty Turnbull and Olga, Jimmy Dey and Alice, Pat and Vera Lennox, 'The Two Harlequins', and Deveen.

In his Newcastle dressing room Gonella's hopes were raised by a flood of good-luck messages and telegrams. One came from a professional boxer friend. 'I got knocked out last night,' it read. 'You knock them out tonight. Red.' And once on-stage, the Georgians – Pat Smuts (tenor), Harold 'Babe' Hood (piano), Jimmy Messini (guitar and vocals), Charlie Winter, not to be confused (as he frequently was) with Tiny Winters (double bass), and Bob Dryden (drums) – did exactly that, sending both audiences wild with delight. In those days performers were sometimes paid – as they are today – by 'house percentage' and this was the case at Newcastle. Nat summed up his overnight success in typically down-to-earth fashion. 'Yes,' he said, 'everything clicked! Everybody came – and we made a lot of money. I came out of it with about £375 for my whack. Not bad, was it?' Later he told Sheila Tracy: '[After Newcastle] I had three more weeks: Nottingham, Liverpool and Birmingham, and after that they wanted to put me on wages: "No; I'll stick to percentage if you don't mind!"' This was unsurprising. Trumpeter Bruce Adams (a Gonella protégé) says that, in his 1930s peak years, Gonella regularly earned a staggering seven hundred pounds a week.

Despite such casual utterances, Gonella planned his stage-act meticulously. The Georgians dressed, American college-boy fashion, in white flannel trousers and striped blazers decorated with unique badges on the breast pocket, featuring the initials 'NG' above an image of the instrument of the sideman concerned. Before the curtains parted, audiences would hear Nat's trumpet playing 'Georgia on My Mind' without accompaniment. 'He would stick the bell of his trumpet through the curtains,' remembers lifelong fan John Wortham, 'just the bell, and play "Georgia" ending on a terrific high note, as the curtains pulled across. It was fantastically effective for those days.'

The remainder of the programme was also planned carefully, Lew Stone-style, to please as many music fans as possible. A swing tune such as 'Sweet Sue' would be followed by a comedy piece – 'I Can't Dance (I Got Ants in My Pants)' – then a jazz selection such as 'Basin Street Blues' and, of course, a spectacular finale on 'Tiger Rag'. This last remained a firm favourite in the Georgians' programme; Nat, a lifelike tiger draped round his neck, would throw smaller soft toy tigers concealed in the piano out into the auditorium. This was an expensive exercise as (understandably) few of the lucky recipients would throw their souvenir back on-stage, although daughter Natalie remembers doing the honest thing by her father on at least one occasion! Above all, the emphasis was on showmanship and snappy music delivered at a hectic pace. 'There was always something moving,' Gonella explained later. 'We never claimed to be a one hundred per cent jazz act. Probably only thirty-five per cent of it was jazz; we were a variety act first and foremost on the stage, and commercial was the name of the game.'

The Georgians' basic line-up (despite changes for recording purposes) remained happy and stable for all of its four-year existence, until the Second World War. Drummer Bob Dryden, born in Leeds, Yorkshire, in 1902, was of course the senior member. An ex-RAF musician, he had left the service in 1926 to form his own band, which played residencies in Britain and at the Majestic Hotel in Bombay, India. Later he worked with Dave Crook's band in London and with the Georgians, as part of Lew Stone's show. He was (possibly) a steadying influence on his youthful comrades although recognised off-stage as a regular drinker.

Pianist Harold 'Babe' Hood, the son of a Great Western Railway official, was born in Newport, Monmouth, in 1917 and was only eighteen when he became a full-time Georgian. Something of a prodigy, he began teaching himself the piano at four-years-old and subsequently worked in several London bands including subbing for a British legend, the great nightclub pianist Gerry Moore at the Bag O' Nails Club, where Nat spotted him. In future years he would justify Nat's faith in him as a superstar of British swing and maintained a long career in music until the early 1980s.

Tenorist Pat Smuts, born in Johannesburg in 1913, had come to Britain from South Africa in a band led by the British comedian Charles Heslop, with whom he worked in Yorkshire in 1931. A year later Smuts moved to London, toured with Louis Armstrong in 1932, and then worked with bands led by drummer Sid Heiger (at the Bag O' Nails), Ord Hamilton (1934) and Howard Jacobs before joining Nat Gonella in 1935. A powerful tenorist whose style naturally recalled Coleman Hawkins and Chu Berry, the handsome Smuts continued his career after the war with the Skyrockets (1945–55) and was still active as a musician in the 1980s when, now re-married, he toured and recorded with Digby Fairweather's *Tribute to Nat* show, carrying on playing gigs for several years thereafter.

Singer/guitarist Jimmy Messini (born 6 March 1908) was quite another matter. Even his name is in some doubt and has sometimes been given as Mesene. A flamboyant personality, he claimed, at various times, to be the son of either a Maltese millionaire or a wealthy Greek shipping magnate. He similarly claimed to have obtained a BSc at Taunton University; presumably in languages, as he could speak seven of them. One of his features, 'Black Eyes', was rendered in Russian and when a critical listener claimed that his Russian pronunciation was poor, Messini retorted sharply that he was, in fact, singing the song in Greek. Before a show he would loosen his voice backstage with 'mi-mi-mi' exercises and a throat-clearing cough and on one occasion his mischievous fellow sidemen told him that Caruso, the legendary tenor, always drank a raw egg in sherry before a performance. Messini immediately went in search of supplies, returning triumphantly with a dozen eggs and a full bottle of sherry, of which the Georgians drank half before topping up the bottle with water and blowing the eggs. Messini was quite justifiably furious, particularly as he regularly drank before performing.

Jimmy Messini was something of an anachronism among the jazz-based Georgians. He attracted criticism from fans, and Nat Gonella himself had difficulty in persuading Parlophone to record his vocals. Today, it must be admitted that he sounds strained and archaic, but Nat told Ron Brown that Messini came into his own on-stage and was always well received by live audiences, despite a tendency to forget words and throw in an alcoholically-prompted operatic adaptation of scat-singing instead.

Double bassist Charlie Winter was a similarly colourful character. Born two years before Nat Gonella, in 1906 in Berwick-on-Tweed, he was the son of a musician in the King's Own Scottish Borderers, killed at Gallipoli. As his mother served as a nurse throughout the First World War, Charlie was sent to the Queen Victoria School in Dunblane, where he was taught music and rapidly became competent on flute, baritone horn and euphonium. At fourteen he joined the 11th Hussars as a bandsman and served in Egypt playing euphonium, tenor horn and bass trombone before taking up the double bass. After 1930 he played with a variety of bands, including Alan Green, Bobby Hinds and his Sonora Band, Teddy Foster and Lou Simmons' Café Anglais band before joining Gonella's Georgians in 1935. He was active in music until the 1950s, when he joined the Shell Oil Company, but returned to Britain in the 1980s for a reunion with his old trumpeter-boss.

Nat Gonella's Georgians to some degree set a pattern for high-profile small groups that broke away from big bands: groups like Joe Daniels and his Hot Shots (formed from members of Harry Roy's band) and Harry Gold and his Pieces of Eight (from members of Oscar Rabin's) are examples. The Georgians themselves, after their successful Newcastle debut, instantly turned into a premier attraction. Variety bookings flooded in and Parlophone record dates numbered at least two a month. Unfortunately, however, Gonella – like many bandleaders of the day – opted for one-off cash payments for sessions rather than longer-term royalty arrangements. In later years he regretted the regular re-appearance of his recordings without remuneration (although one or two honourable latter-day producers offered welcome payments). At the time, after the Georgians had been paid, Nat would normally earn about seventy-five pounds for a session; fees that might easily be gambled away the same day. 'I lost a fortune to Ladbrokes,' he told Digby Fairweather later. The money must have been considerable: during 1935 the Georgians recorded forty-eight sides for Parlophone – in current parlance, two singles a month.

Such records normally received favourable reviews despite the determined efforts of a few critics to belittle the Georgians. Leonard Feather – soon to become an important part of America's jazz scene as commentator, author, pianist and composer and in later years something of a legend – was scornful of Gonella's recorded output at the time. Writing for *Swing Music* in June 1935, Feather said,

> Play Nat Gonella's 'Tiger Rag' after hearing an average American busking band (Manone or Prima) if you want to appreciate what a lamentable effort it is. The tempo is absurdly fast, the melody instruments do not blend well and make no attempt to co-ordinate. The showmanship and scat-singing sounds insincere and meaningless, the solos and hot breaks are neither original in style nor technically clever; even Nat himself is undistinguished. It is a typical result of what happens to a good artist when he becomes a commercial success. Heaven help hot music!

Feather – young, ambitious and bound for American residency for much of his life – was highly opinionated, as well as fashion-conscious, and not above laying into American artists on their home territory a few years later. The legendary Eddie Condon and cornettist Muggsy Spanier were among his victims, the latter dedicating a title, 'Feather Brain Blues', to the writer. Nevertheless, Nat Gonella was doing very nicely for a British-born jazzman. In a poll conducted by *Swing Music* (the magazine in which Feather's vilification appeared) he was placed number one as 'Britain's favourite soloist', and third in a world poll after Louis Armstrong and Coleman Hawkins.

Despite Feather's opinion of 'Tiger Rag', fans loved it. Parlophone Records themselves adopted the tiger motif and used a photograph of Nat, a toy tiger draped around his neck, in its record lists. On one extra-musical occasion, however, the tiger came in for a severe beating. Gonella was a wrestling fan in the days when the sport was genuinely a bone-breaker and fights were not choreographed as in later years. During one bout he attended at ringside, a mountainous grappler called the 'Tiger' was coming in for a severe beating from his opponent, and Nat sought to offer encouragement by throwing one of his toy tigers into the ring. The wrestler, on spotting it, took his wrath out on the toy, ripping it to pieces and sending its white stuffing flying. Nat promptly changed his rooting allegiances to the opposing wrestler!

One of the Georgians' earlier records, 'Oh Peter', is said to have been issued in error with a misspelled title by Parlophone. According to Gonella, the song was of Scandinavian origin and written about a young woman called Peta; otherwise, in Gonella's matter-of-fact words, 'I would have been singing a love song to a bloke!' Although this would have been controversial in 1935 (Gonella's version was recorded in October of that year), the issue is debatable. 'Oh Peter' was first recorded by Billy Banks and his Rhythmakers in April 1932 with the same spelling and Banks was a noted gay entertainer. 'Peter' is also black slang for a penis. This was not the only controversy over record company titles. Two years later, Gonella's cover version of Louis Armstrong's 'Skeleton in the Closet' was discreetly changed to 'Skeleton in the Cupboard' as Parlophone understood that in Britain 'closet' implied 'lavatory'. These were innocent times and in 1935 the BBC banned scat-singing. Gonella wrote to ask why the corporation had taken such a decision and received the vague explanation that the ban had been imposed after listeners' complaints. This was not to be his last skirmish with the BBC.

As Britain's premier hot trumpeter, Nat was a role-model for hundreds of aspiring trumpeters, and accordingly he produced both demonstration records and a trumpet tutor. The records, coupling 'Tiger Rag' and 'When You're Smiling', are described by one of Gonella's most ardent fans of the period: 'The record companies used to put out accompaniment records for the assistance of beginners like myself,' recalled Humphrey Lyttelton*. 'The first side of the record consisted of oom-cha rhythm accompaniments with the occasional piano passage to give struggling chops a rest. The reverse sides... had Nat Gonella dubbing his own solos over the same accompaniment to demonstrate key modulations, breaks and hot improvisation. For all that, there are some good bits of jazz trumpet, especially on "When You're Smiling".'

Gonella's tutor *Modern Style Trumpet Playing: A Comprehensive Course*, published by Henri Selmer, remains an interesting and now collectable volume. Dedicated 'To Louis Armstrong, King of Trumpeters' and published in hardback, it was divided into two sections: 'Groundwork' (breathing, attack and articulation, tone cultivation, major and minor scales, tonguing, vibrato and more) and 'Modern Style'. This second section – well in advance of its time – dealt with mutes, tricks, fake fingering, high notes, extemporising and elementary harmony (including chords, chord-scales, blue notes and much else), phrasing and chorus building and 'playing in the dance

* in his sleevenote to an early Gonella LP reissue, *The Georgia Boy from London*.

band'. Although in all probability the book was ghost-written, Gonella's likeable informality and no-nonsense approach strongly suggest that he contributed all the source material to begin with. And although not everything his tutor contains has remained current, it is still a useful and stimulating instruction manual. Readers who absorbed its teaching include two fine latter-day British jazz trumpeters, Humphrey Lyttelton and John Chilton.

During the 1930s Gonella lost money both at the racetrack and in unsuccessful business ventures. One such involved bankrolling a West End shop which sold only shirts. Drummer Jim Byrne recalls that the trumpeter told him, 'I handed a roll of notes to the manager, as it seemed like a good idea. But then I went off on tour and when I got back I went to the shop and it had "Closed" across the front and a "For Sale" sign up!' Gonella told Byrne that his chagrin increased when, a few months later, he was asked to reinvest in the project.

Then as now, a good car was a necessity for a travelling musician and even at that time motoring around the country from venue to venue offered its share of risks. On one occasion, driving from Wales to the Midlands with passenger Bob Dryden, Nat suffered a head-on collision with another vehicle at a road junction. His car was written-off but miraculously he and Dryden escaped all major injury. After the wreckage was towed away Nat shrugged his shoulders. 'Well,' he said, 'I guess it was just my unlucky day.' It was; he had already been stopped by police in Cardiff for speeding that morning.

Another time, the Georgians played a Sunday concert at Stoke-on-Trent and stayed the night there before driving on to Bradford's Alhambra for a week in variety. They left Stoke at 11.30 next morning but within the hour Harold Hood's car developed engine trouble and Pat Smuts offered to stay with the pianist while the rest of the Georgians drove on, Bob Dryden with Nat, and Jimmy Messini riding with Charlie Winter. On the way, Nat turned left at a crossroads but Winter missed the turning and drove straight on. Nat turned round, only to be passed by his sidemen coming the other way. Then a thick fog came down, forcing Nat to walk ahead of the car while Dryden manned the wheel, and finally the two unfortunate travellers crawled into Sheffield. The fog, however, showed no sign of clearing, and their journey was continued by train. Tired, hungry and dirty, Gonella and Dryden finally arrived at the Bradford Alhambra at nine o'clock – too late for the evening's performance. The leader's dark mood was aggravated when he discovered that Winter and the rest of his band had somehow missed the fog and arrived comfortably enough in Bradford by 3.30 in the afternoon.

Harold Hood, youngest of the Georgians, was always keen to learn to drive and persuaded Charlie Winter, previously his on-tour chauffeur, to give him driving lessons in a brand-new Baby Austin. Hood was nervous, so it was decided that the lessons would take place on country roads. Even in calm rural surroundings, the would-be driver at one point stamped on his accelerator by accident and his car hurtled through a hedge into a field occupied by a great black bull, which accelerated towards them while Hood desperately struggled to find reverse gear. In his panic, Winter jumped on to the pianist's lap to operate the pedals. They reversed out of trouble in the nick of time, while the offended bull snorted angrily through his hedge at the invaders.

Driving and drinking could produce problems. Both Bob Dryden and Jimmy Messini were spirits drinkers, and after the band had finished their show would find a local club with a bar which stayed open into the small hours. Messini would regularly ring Charlie Winter and ask him to drive Dryden back to his home in Morden. On one occasion Winter obligingly did this in his own car, leaving Dryden's in a local garage. Next day the bassist received an angry phone call from his passenger, whose wife had hauled her husband over the coals for both arriving home late, and mislaying their car.

Domestic disputes such as this did little to slow up the band's drinking. Soon after, when the Georgians were starring at the Dominion Theatre, Tottenham Court Road, Dryden had taken delivery of a brand-new car, but nevertheless drank deep after the show. Despite pleas from the band, he drove away, mounted a road island and smashed a traffic bollard. The car needed extensive repairs and for a week afterwards Dryden sported a black eye. His fellow musicians were never sure if this was a result of the crash or of his wife's mounting fury at her husband's on-the-road misadventures.

Around this time, *Popular Music* magazine told its readers that horse-riding was becoming a favoured pastime for top bandleaders, including Henry Hall, Jack Payne, Harry Roy – and Nat Gonella. 'This was a novel twist,' Ron Brown later observed, 'Nat putting his backside on a gee-gee instead of his shirt.' But Gonella, like many of his fellow bandleaders (in particular Ambrose) had been attracted to gambling and horses from early in his career. Brown asked Gonella the maximum amount he had ever lost on a bet during the 1930s. 'Four hundred pounds,' replied the trumpeter, with a rueful smile.

Bob Dryden also developed a passion for horse-riding and one day asked Charlie Winter, a keen photographer, to take a picture of him making a jump on horseback. The ever-obliging Winter did so, lying – at Dryden's suggestion – behind the fence to achieve a good aerial effect. Unfortunately Dryden's horse, sensing a presence, came to a shuddering halt and, minus horse, Dryden made the jump alone. Amid the shock Winter forgot to press his shutter anyhow.

Supplementing his passion for horses and horseracing, Nat was often to be found at greyhound stadiums around the country. Several prominent bandleaders owned both dogs and horses and Gonella, at one point, owned two official G.R. (Greyhound Racing) organisation dogs. One of these, called Great Relief (a possible reference back to the initials of the organisation concerned) was a useful runner and near-unbeatable if it hit the front of the pack early on, and then stuck to the inside rail. At one meeting, however, Nat was advised by his trainer that Great Relief stood no chance; it was running against two bigger dogs who, starting from traps on either side, would crowd his dog into a losing central course. This sounded like good advice and Nat placed ten pounds on the favourite to win. Contrary to expectation, Great Relief came out of the trap like a rocket, made for the inside rail and beat all opposition to the winning post, despite its owners vote of no confidence.

Late in 1935 the Georgians embarked on a short but successful tour of Holland. Returning to the country as a solo star after his successful visit with Ray Noble four years before gave Nat genuine pleasure, and a friendly Dutch impresario whom he had met during the Noble visit arranged concerts in premier venues. After one of these the visiting stars were invited to meet local dignitaries, who had a presentation ready for them. The Georgians lined up on stage at the end of the show, and each of them was given a small Gouda cheese! They made friends with Holland's top jazz orchestra, the Ramblers, and, considering their popularity in Holland, it was a small irony that the British group was destined ultimately to break up there.

The Georgians were extremely popular in Europe. Tenorist Pat Smuts later told Ron Brown: 'Yes, they were marvellous times; the best years of my life. There would be amazing scenes wherever we played, especially when we toured abroad, with hordes of fans gathering outside our hotel chanting for Nat to make an appearance on the balcony. We were treated like royalty – it was Beatlemania [nearly] thirty years before the Beatles!'

Throughout the 1930s Nat appeared in several films. These included *Sing as You Swing* (1937), an eighty-two minute musical directed by Redd Davis, in which the theme concerned competing radio stations and music was provided by Gonella's Georgians and his friends the Mills Brothers. Later it was cut into two versions, renamed *Swing Tease* and *The Music Box*. Other films included *Variety Parade*, *Here's Health* (actually a short commercial for Beecham's powders and pills) and the very first of Gonella's bandleading appearances on film from 1935, a twenty-two minute short directed by Ian Walker, distributed by Associated British Films Ltd and titled *Pity the Poor Rich*. The film's press publicity promised 'a full measure of lively hot-cha syncopations by Nat Gonella and his merry Georgians, songs by Queenie Leonard, a dash of comedy, juggling, and a spice of romance in the story of a young couple's evening out combining… to furnish diversity of entertainment rarely found in the compass of a two-reel offering.' In a nightclub setting, Nat and his Georgians in their Lew Stone incarnation (including Albert Torrance, Monia Liter, Ernie Ritte, Don Barrigo and Tiny Winters) play four numbers featuring their leader: 'Georgia on My Mind', 'I'm Gonna Wash My Hands of You', 'Troublesome Trumpet' and 'Tiger Rag'.

Pity the Poor Rich is no masterpiece (it contains the conventional silly-ass Englishman declaring to his escort, 'We can't dance to this'), but it should be remembered that 'talkies' were still a comparative novelty, and this one vividly captures Gonella's high-powered act which, after all, is really the reason for its existence.

The film opens outside the entrance of a plush hotel; the Georgians enter from the right pushing a large sports car with Nat sitting inside. They are calling, 'Heave, heave!' and the dialogue continues:

Boys in the Band: 'We can't push this any further!'

Nat: 'No.' Turning to chauffeur: 'Run along to the garage and fetch some petrol.'

Chauffeur: 'Yes sir.'

Boys in the band: 'Queer name for a hotel!'

Nat: 'Oh, it's called the "Hotel Encore" because all the top variety stars stay here.'

Boys in the band: 'Well, they will appreciate a bit of good music then.'

Nat: 'Sure, come on boys, we'll rehearse the new number, the classical one!'

On cue, they launch into a tear-up rendition of 'Tiger Rag' (further enlivened by a Torrance solo for which, as he recalled to Digby Fairweather in 2002, 'The producer wanted all high notes – so I had to play right up in the Ds, Es and Fs'). *Popular Music* noted that 'Nat Gonella and his band made a bright appearance' in the film. In its July issue the magazine nominated their ideal all-star British 'band of bandleaders': Nat Gonella and Jack Jackson (trumpets), Roy Fox (cornet), Harry Roy and Howard Jacobs (saxophones), Ambrose and Sydney Lipton (violins), Lou Preager (accordion), Henry Hall (piano), Jack Payne (piano, vocals) and Billy Cotton (drums).

The Georgians continued to pack theatres (including the

London Palladium) throughout 1936 and recorded fifty-seven more titles for Parlophone including 'Woe Is Me', 'Crazy Valves' and 'His Old Cornet'. By now Gonella was seen as not just a Louis Armstrong echo but a star in his own right, and one 1936 edition of *Rhythm Magazine* even accused the black trumpeter Teddy Foster of being a Gonella copyist. It summed up by saying that although Foster was one of the better imitators, he lacked Gonella's exuberance.

As Nat's popularity grew, a fan club was formed to cater for a growing army of followers. Members received an enamel club badge and copies of a monthly newsletter *The Georgian*, a bright, cheerful publication detailing the latest news on the band's datesheet and new recordings, plus a lively 'readers' column'. The club and magazine were run by Douglas Graf; Nat himself was styled 'Honorary President' and the vice-president was Betty Gonella. By early 1937 the club had about five hundred members and, of these, number 189 was one Beryl Bryden from Norwich. After the war Bryden would begin a lifelong career as a professional singer and star of the post-war traditional jazz movement. Known as 'Britain's Queen of the Blues', she still kept a complete collection of Gonella's records in the 1980s and maintained a friendship with the trumpeter up until her death in 1998. She also recorded with him – notably for Ted Easton in 1970 and on a last recording date with Igor Bourco's Uralsky Jazzmen in 1997 for the CD *Oh! Mo'nah*.

Another of Gonella's fans was John Wortham who recalled:

> I was at school with racing driver Donald Campbell, later tragically killed on Coniston Water, and he really inspired my enthusiasm for Nat. Taciturn by nature, Donald was, however, a passionate Gonella devotee. In those pre-war days it was possible to order records direct from the factory and my father, bless him, arranged for EMI to send me the latest Gonella releases each month. As

these arrived three weeks before being available in the shops, this made me highly popular at school.

I met Nat quite a few times as a young fan but didn't get to know him until 1970. His stage shows were legendary, with presentation and movement paramount. There was always the business with the tigers: throwing them into the audience and sometimes the gag with mummy and daddy tiger in the piano and the string of cubs at the end! Always a snappy dresser, he insisted on at least three dress changes per show for the Georgians. And he was a kind and generous man – even when he was a superstar in the 1930s and 1940s he always replied to letters from fans, so unlike many of his contemporaries.

In the years leading up to 1939 the Georgians played the London Palladium several times, and for one of their more unusual appearances – in the week commencing 17 August 1936 – shared the bill with American comedian/actor Joe E. Brown. Brown had no stage act but assured the theatre management there was no cause for concern; as long as there was a band in the show he would improvise a routine with them. On opening night, turn number five featured Lucan and McShane (Old Mother Riley and her daughter Kitty) followed by Nat Gonella's Georgians and then – top of the bill – the large-mouthed comedian himself. Brown opened with comedy patter and then borrowed a baton from Gonella for a hilarious routine in which he 'conducted' the Georgians. Nat caught on quickly and acted as the perfect stooge, to the audience's delight; the routine stayed in place for the week's run. Two years later, in May 1938, Nat and his Georgians were top of the bill; supporting acts included veteran ventriloquist Arthur Prince and dummy Jim, American singing star Harry Richman, and comedians Will Hay and Max Wall.

By 1938 the Georgians had been joined by Malaysian singer Stella Moya, who before joining Gonella had cherished the hopes of a would-be film 'starlet' and made one brief appearance on film with comedians Bud Flanagan and Chesney Allen. Although a no-more-than competent singer, Moya was visually stunning; an Oriental beauty who, said *Rhythm Magazine*, 'would appeal to any red-blooded male in the audience.' 'We were all in love with Stella Moya before the war,' recalls Britain's premier jazz agent, Jack Higgins. 'She looked exactly like Dorothy Lamour.' Nat, displaying his sense of showmanship (and sexual taste) made the most of her looks: before she appeared for the first time the stage would be blacked out. Then a solitary pin-spot would pick out Moya at side of the stage as she sang, 'It's a Sin to Tell a Lie' at ballad tempo, before – halfway through the number – Nat and the Georgians would pick up the tempo to bring the music to a jumping conclusion. As her musical confidence grew, Stella recorded sides with Gonella's band at Parlophone's studios including 'Boo Hoo' (21 April 1937), 'Toodle-oo' and 'Take Another Guess' (2 July 1937).

Late in 1936 Nat toured the number-one Moss Empire circuit with a show called *South American Joe*, which began its run at the Brighton Hippodrome and went on to play most of Britain's biggest theatres. The cast enjoyed dressing up in both cowboy and Mexican rig, rather as the Busby Boys had done years earlier and, in addition to the Georgians and their leader, the show featured Phyllis Robins, a talented singer who had previously worked with Billy Cotton, Jack Hylton, Ambrose and Carroll Gibbons. One song she helped to popularise was 'Me and My Dog (Lost in a Fog)', written by Vivian Ellis in 1936 for the film *Public Nuisance No.1*.

Comedian Al Burnett and American xylophonist Teddy Brown also appeared in the show. Brown, a remarkable presence on the variety circuits of the 1930s and 1940s, had trained as a classical musician, but eventually turned to dance music and formed his own band. He first appeared in Britain at the Café de Paris and the Kit Kat Club and then began working the halls as a top attraction. After demonstrating his extraordinary virtuosity early on in his act, the forbidding-looking Brown – weighing well over twenty stone and seventy-five inches around the waist – would bark at his audience: 'Sing!' They sang! Despite his menacing appearance and huge girth, Brown appeared in one *South American Joe* scene dressed as a cowboy, complete with stetson hat three feet in diameter. The xylophonist was prone to the giggles and one night laughed so hard that he fell over backwards and could not get up again. Eventually the curtain was rung down leaving a hysterical audience with the parting view of Nat and his company struggling to lift their star back to an upright position. Brown died in 1946, in his mid-forties.

As a superstar of his day, Nat Gonella was naturally a target for magazines and gossip columnists who regularly delved into his private life. Their enquiries, however, were generally far less intrusive than those of twenty-first century tabloids. In one 1936 edition of *Rhythm*, critic Edgar Jackson featured Nat's daughter Natalie in an article headlined 'Tailor's Apprentice to Trumpet Ace'. Natalie was pictured posing with her father and the band while playing a toy trumpet. In the same year *Radio Pictorial*'s more personal feature was titled 'The girls that want to marry me!' It revealed that Britain's top trumpet star received sackfuls of fan mail, most of it from female admirers. Some letters were highly intimate, prompting a request from Nat that they should stop. While he was happy to write about his playing, records and broadcasts, Gonella declared that he could not handle letters from lovelorn girls. He made it clear that he was happily married to Betty (who as secretary of his club answered much of the mail) and adored his daughter.

Nat's assertion that his marriage was happy was no longer altogether true; his relationship was under considerable strain. A fourteen-hour working day, extensive touring over six years, the pressures of stardom – all were likely to take their toll. And the first signs of a marriage breakdown appeared on 23 September 1936 when Betty sailed to America on the S.S. *Normandie*. She would not be back in England until 13 January 1937; a fifteen-week pleasure trip covering both Christmas and New Year. This was a blow for young Natalie who also missed the birthday she shared with her mother; on 8 October Betty was twenty-eight and her daughter six. In 2002 Natalie Gonella (now Natalie Wilson) talked about the marriage and its problems: 'Nat and Betty really were children when they got married. My father was twenty-two and I was born on my mother's twenty-second birthday. But she really was a very fun-loving girl. She loved the stardom and the high life. And that long trip to America was one example of how much she liked a good time. Of course my father was also at the peak of his fame so maybe things went wrong there too. Who knows?' In 1936, in a poignant letter to the Gonella fan club, accompanying a Christmas message, six-year-old Natalie wrote from Shaftesbury High School in Dorset to explain that she was living in the country with her grandmother. The letter mentioned her pet dog Bill, confirmed that she missed her mother and father very much and concluded by saying that, although the little girl appreciated the big doll's house and bicycle Nat had given her for Christmas, 'I hope my Daddy will come here soon to see me. We have such fun together.'

To all intents and purposes Gonella's first marriage was over. He had fallen in love with the irresistible Stella Moya, in the wake of a marriage in which his first wife was arguably more at fault than he. Unusually, in fact, for the period (as possibly today) Nat, rather than his wife Betty, was granted custody of daughter Natalie. Today she remembers her childhood:

> Following his divorce from Betty in 1937, Nat was surprised and somewhat embarrassed to be granted custody of me – especially as the band was still on tour and there was really no settled home life to offer a seven year old. Then of course there was a new girlfriend who didn't particularly want me around! I spent a few weeks at Nat's home in Edgware and then visited various friends for short spells until both Betty's mother, Grandma Alice Stride, and sister Ray, who was an absolute angel, took it in turns to look after me in various parts of the country.
>
> Grandma Alice – a very well-spoken and educated lady like my mother – was housekeeper to a Major Griffin at Bourne Hall, in Bourne, Cambridgeshire. But she died quite early of dropsy, which was a horrid disease and harrowing to watch. I would have been about ten or eleven at the time and after that Ray took over and she was fantastic! – A red-head who smoked like a chimney, a brilliant linguist and she played wonderful piano too, reading music or by ear. Anything from classics to even a bit of jazz. I think that's why Nat was as close to her as he was. Ray would take me to the movies, as she loved films – and she played for the silent movies too in the period before talkies came along.

However, the young girl missed her father and extravagant gifts were no substitute for paternal visits. Natalie recalls:

> Betty was by now enjoying a new glamorous life and soon lost regular touch. Nat had little opportunity to visit and, once he went abroad with the army and with new ladies in his life, it was some long while before we saw each other; a fact he much regretted, I think, as he missed my growing-up. Later in life though, really after he decided to make a go of it with Dorothy, we saw much more of each other. By that time, of course, his life had slowed down rather, and regular phone calls helped us to get to know and

love each other again. But, if you want my opinion, Stella was really the love of his life. He adored her and was heartbroken when she left him in the end.

Moya also became more involved with the everyday work of the Georgians, a fact resented by certain band members who saw her – with a mixture of jealousy and natural musicians' cynicism – as an outsider with bandleader privileges which she was exploiting. The situation is far from unique in bandleading circles: four years earlier, American drummer Ben Pollack's romance with singer Doris Robbins had seen the end of the Pollack organisation and the successful start of the Bob Crosby organisation. Nothing so drastic would happen with the Georgians, but Bob Dryden and Jimmy Messini spoke angrily of the situation in small-hours drinking sessions.

Touring continued unabated. One night the Georgians might be playing a city theatre and the next a village hall. Nat Gonella's own most vivid memories concerned dates in the north of England where poverty was at its most hopeless. At one show in Northumberland, the concert hall was at first half-empty, then gradually filled to capacity while the lights were down. When the lights went up for the interval the trumpeter was amazed to see that every member of the audience was apparently in blackface. This was a mining town and the audience was composed of miners who took their seats in the hall as they were released from their differing shifts. After the show he met the booking agent, who showed the trumpeter a thick wad of payment cards; his audience had paid threepence a week from their wages for several months to see Gonella's Georgians. Nat was moved and humbled.

Scottish dates were memorable too, especially in Glasgow, a notoriously risky arena for acts – especially those from the south of England. (It was famously said of audiences at

Glasgow Empire, 'If they like you they let you live!') One night the Georgians were booked to play at a dance hall in the Barrowland district of the city, so called for its street-market area and tough inhabitants. At this time, when the venue allowed, the band had an effective way of opening their session: Nat would stroll towards his on-stage Georgians through the auditorium in a pin-spot, playing 'Georgia on My Mind'. On this occasion, however, a roomful of unforgiving faces adorned with razor scars gave the normally tough leader second thoughts. Not so the management, who liked the idea and promised a bodyguard. As the show began Nat strolled across the dancefloor surrounded – and dwarfed – by six former heavyweight boxers. On arrival at the stage he went into his act and completed it while his six minders stood at front-stage, arms folded.

While in Scotland the Georgians also played a late show at Stirling. As they had already played a full show elsewhere that evening and the second could not start until 2 a.m., Gonella felt sure that only a handful of people would be present. When they arrived, however, the hall was jammed and disappointed crowds were waiting for tickets. 'It was just as well that Nat and the band bothered to get there,' a commentator observed, 'otherwise the organisers of the show probably would have been lynched.'

Newcastle was another interesting northern booking – particularly for bassist Charlie Winter. The boarding-house in which he stayed overlooked the city's football ground and Winter climbed through the roof hatch to get a good view of the match. After the final whistle blew, he returned to the hatch to find that it had fallen back down and could be opened only from the inside. Banging on it and shouting himself hoarse produced no results until, at last, his landlady noticed her guest's absence and climbed the stairs to investigate. Hearing shouts for help she located Winter and opened the hatch in time to allow him to race to the Empire Theatre and join the Georgians for their show.

When touring abroad, the band usually stayed in five-star hotels, but theatrical digs around Britain were less reliable. During a week at the Liverpool Empire a convention of Roman Catholic priests was in town for the opening of the new cathedral and hotel rooms were at a premium. Charlie Winter managed to find lodgings in a down-at-heel house in Upper Parliament Street. As the week progressed he noticed that certain personal items – toothpaste and shaving soap – were mysteriously disappearing. Then, returning to his room on a chance errand, he was astounded to find a Chinese man sleeping in his bed. As Charlie didn't use his room in the day, explained his landlady, she had assumed that he would not mind the man, a night-worker, using his bed during the day. After telling his hostess what he thought of her, Winter moved to Birkenhead to stay with friends.

For the Georgians, filling in daytime hours in a strange town could be boring. Pat Smuts and Charlie Winter often visited the local golf course; Smuts was a fine golfer but Winter admitted later that he 'only went along for the walk'. The two musicians often played threesomes with comedian Ted Ray, a skilled golfer. During one round Pat drove off with a fine stroke but, to the players' perplexity, his ball seemed to drop suddenly. On reaching the spot they discovered that it had hit and killed a blackbird. Ray consoled Smuts with the observation that his shot had at least produced a 'birdie'.

Back in London the Georgians continued recording apace and, through 1937, cut sixty-two sides. Included were jazz and swing hits (for example 'Caravan', 'Peckin'' and 'I'm Getting

Sentimental Over You'), novelty specials such as 'I'd Like to See Samoa of Samoa' and 'My Swiss Hill-Billy', and (for Moya) a cover version of a song featured by Virginia O'Brien in *The Harvey Girls*, 'Oh, They're Tough, Mighty Tough in the West' (2 September 1937). One other unusual recording at the period was with George Formby for a song called 'Doh-de-oh-Doh'. (Formby had been employed in one of Gonella's stage-shows while Nat – as top-of-the-bill attraction – took the risk of a percentage take.)

Whatever their character, most popular titles on 78 r.p.m. records were aimed at a dance market and had to have an appropriate tempo for dancing purposes. Labels including 'Quickstep', 'Foxtrot', or 'Rhumba' reminded even hot jazz fans that music was played for dancing as well as for listening. At Abbey Road studios, no less an authority than dance expert and ballroom maestro Victor Sylvester was employed to advise Gonella and his band on the correct tempo for selections.

As 1937 made way for 1938 Nat Gonella and his Georgians began another year which would bring the group yet more acclaim in Britain and abroad. Though nobody was aware of it at the time, it would also be the band's last full year together.

6

*The Big Apple**

In 1938 Nat struck up a friendship with one of jazz history's most colourful legends, Thomas 'Fats' Waller. Waller was touring in variety in Britain and appeared at Brighton Hippodrome in the same week that the Georgians were playing at Sherry's Ballroom nearby. Visiting Sherry's, Fats was persuaded to sit in on an impromptu jam session on 'Honeysuckle Rose', a performance which, by some accounts, lasted up to one hour. Waller was a front-page sensation at this point in his career and everyone in Brighton's musical fraternity heard about the appearance. Unfortunately this included the Hippodrome management, who took a dim view of their star appearing for free at a rival venue and fined Waller fifty pounds. This was a considerable sum; Waller was furious and the tour might have ended there and then if his manager, Ed Kirkeby, had not counselled restraint.

Waller's alcoholic consumption was legendary and one night, after the hotel bar had closed, the pianist invited every-

*Parlophone, Nat Gonella and his Georgians, 24.9.37

one back to his room to keep on drinking. As the session progressed, Nat decided that he had had enough and slipped back to his hotel room. At 3 a.m. he was awakened by the telephone ringing at his bedside. It was Waller. 'Man, where have you been? We've been waiting for you!'

Summer, as usual, brought a heavy schedule for the Georgians because – in addition to variety seasons – they played Sunday concerts, usually in seaside towns. These normally involved two houses: one at three p.m., the second at eight. As many jazz fans attended both concerts, Gonella would change his entire programme for each show. Each included a dozen or so selections in which both Nat and his band had a chance to show off their jazz talents to the full. Pat Smuts often chose 'Shine' for his feature while Harold Hood opted for 'Sweet Sue, Just You'. Nevertheless, the band occasionally ran into trouble over Sunday concerts which set out to feature hot jazz on the Lord's day. At Hanley in Staffordshire, where Gonella played the Odeon Theatre, any Sunday entertainment was frowned on and theatre managers had to apply for a special licence from local magistrates. The manager of the Odeon was required to submit a copy of the Georgians' intended programme and the magistrate took sharp exception to a host of tunes including 'Booglie Wooglie Piggy' and 'Flat Foot Floogie'. By the end of the inquisition, it seemed that not much was left on the page except 'God Save the King'.

Much later, in the 1950s, censorship was still a problem. Humphrey Lyttelton and his band visited a Southend cinema for a Sunday concert and found their programme vetted by a watch committee. All references to holy matters – Lyttelton's programme contained both spirituals and items with religious references – were barred and Lyttelton solved the problem with his customary wit. 'The finale,' he is said to have announced, 'will be "When the Watch Committee Goes Marching in".'

The highlight of Nat Gonella's 1938 summer season, however, was Jack Taylor's seasonal spectacular at Blackpool Hippodrome, *King Revel*. Among its cast of over fifty, the all-star bill included comedian Sandy Powell, Norman Evans, and Duggie Wakefield's Gang along with Gonella's Georgians and Stella Moya. The show was spectacular in best Busby Berkeley style and one scene featured a magnificent glass stairway adorned with beautiful showgirls posing in splendidly colourful costumes. In addition to his band spot with the Georgians, Nat appeared in comedy sketches. Most of the music was specially composed by songwriter Horatio Nicholls. Better known perhaps under his real name of Lawrence Wright, the celebrated music publisher's hits included 'Among My Souvenirs', 'Down Forget-Me-Not Lane' and 'Shepherd of the Hills'. On 16 July Nat took the Georgians into a recording studio to cut a double-sided 78, 'King Revel' and 'The Blackpool Walk', as souvenirs of their stay. Also recorded was Noel Gay's 'The Lambeth Walk', a huge hit for Lupino Lane in his show *Me and My Girl* which was then attracting sell-out audiences at London's Victoria Palace. Seeing its success, Lane sent solicitors' letters to other London producers warning that action would be taken if they used the song in rival productions. While Nat was appearing at the Holloway Gaumont in north London, however, he received a personal letter from Lane assuring him that any such ban was not intended to extend to the trumpeter. He was grateful, he said, to Nat for helping to popularise the song and hoped that the Georgians would carry on playing it.

By Christmas 1938, Nat had been working almost non-stop for four years, and decided that a holiday was in order. He had long dreamed of visiting New York and several American friends had indicated that he would be made welcome. So the decision was made and on 22 December, with Stella Moya, he bade goodbye to the Georgians at Waterloo Station. In a touching gesture of friendship and loyalty they presented him with a gold signet ring before departing to enjoy family Christmases of their own. At Southampton, Nat and Stella boarded the S.S. *Hamburg* for New York.

Nat proved a good sailor but it was not a happy crossing; the weather was atrocious. 'I got quite friendly with the captain,' he told Sheila Tracy. 'All the passengers were Jewish, getting away from the Nazi regime in Germany. I was in first class and there were only about ten of us, all the rest were in steerage.' On the second day, he met Timme Rosenkrantz, a Danish nobleman-turned-journalist who wrote for a music magazine based in Denmark. Rosenkrantz was a lifelong jazz-lover whose activities, at various times, included hosting his own show on New York's Radio WNEW and running his own jam sessions at Café Bohemia where greats such as Bill Coleman, Pete Brown, Joe Thomas and Rex Stewart played. Rosenkrantz also arranged recording sessions for his Barons of Rhythm for Victor, National and Continental. He produced jazz records for many years as well as a now almost legendary book (later re-published by British record-retailer Doug Dobell), his *Swing Photo Album 1939*.

Rosenkrantz was a stimulating companion. He had brought jazz records with him and, after searching the ship for a gramophone on which to play them, the two men discovered that the only one on board was behind a bar. Late at night when the other passengers had retired to their cabins, they crept back to the deserted bar-room to play the records over and over again. On 29 December, New York's skyscraper skyline finally came into view and by the time the liner had docked it was eight in the evening. Nat and Stella hailed a cab to cross the city and check in at the Piccadilly Hotel on West 45th Street, just off Broadway. Some travellers might have opted for an early night in order to begin their explorations of the city next morning, but not Nat Gonella; he had waited a long time for this visit and everything was ahead of him. Filling every waking hour was essential. After a change of clothes, the couple went straight out on the town. First stop was the hotel's Georgia Room to hear bass saxophonist Adrian Rollini. From there they went on to the Paramount to hear Glen Gray's Casa Loma Orchestra with the Andrews Sisters; then the Famous Door on 52nd Street where John Kirby and his band accompanied 'Mr and Mrs. Swing' – Red Norvo and Mildred Bailey. Then, finally, the elated British visitors made their way to Harlem and the Savoy Ballroom where Don Redman shared the stand with the relief band, the Savoy Sultans. Nat remembered later that for him the Sultans, with their outstanding brass section, outshone the main attraction.

Gonella and Stella finally arrived back at their hotel at five in the morning and later that day Nat contacted his old friend, British heavyweight champion Tommy Farr. Welshman Farr was one of only three fighters to have gone the distance with the legendary Joe Louis and, although the 'Brown Bomber' was awarded the fight, the decision was controversial. Farr had remained in America hoping for a return match with Louis, which was not to materialise, but meantime he was in training for a match against Red Burman, a protégé of Jack Dempsey. Nevertheless, he was delighted to see his friend and took him along to Madison Square Gardens to see American boxing in action. Nat went on to the Cotton Club, up in Harlem again, this time to see Cab Calloway's band. Fronted by its showman-leader, rich in hit recordings, Calloway's band was phenomenal. Its stars included altoist Hilton Jefferson, tenorist 'Chu' Berry and drummer Cozy Cole, one of America's greatest (he later worked with Louis Armstrong's All Stars and co-ran a drum school in New York with Gene Krupa). The orchestra also provided the musical backdrop for a two-hour floorshow provided by the Nicholas Brothers, the Dandridge Sisters, the Berry Brothers, Sister Rosetta Tharpe and the 'father of the blues', the legendary W. C. Handy. Almost blind, Handy had to be led on-stage to play trumpet on his own composition 'St Louis Blues'. This night, Gonella's festivities concluded at four in the morning.

In the late 1930s vaudeville was enjoying a temporary revival in America and early on New Year's Eve Nat went to a show starring his old drinking companion Fats Waller. Gonella found Waller much more impressive than he had previously in Britain. Later that night, to celebrate New Year, he and Stella visited the Waldorf Astoria Hotel where Benny Goodman and his orchestra were starring. As the night went on, they met Goodman, pianist Teddy Wilson, vibraphonist Lionel Hampton and trumpeter Harry James. James was 'a very natural fella you know; tall, very quietly spoken,' Nat told Digby Fairweather in the 1990s. 'And he gave me one of his mouthpieces [a Pardubah five-star cushion-rim] that the firm he was advertising for gave him. And I thought, "You keep trying different mouthpieces, but if that's good enough for James, it's good enough for me. So I stuck to it – and I've still got it!"' (Gonella played it for the rest of his career.) At one other point in the evening, he met Lionel Hampton standing by a lift. 'I asked why he was waiting,' Gonella told Sheila Tracy, 'and he said he was waiting for the bell to ring to let him know it was time to go upstairs to play. He wasn't allowed to sit on the stand with the band.'

From the Waldorf, Nat travelled back to Harlem to see Jimmie Lunceford's orchestra at the Renaissance Ballroom. 'I heard him at four o'clock in the morning,' he told Fairweather. 'He'd just started the gig at three! I went down there, the second wife and I, to hear [trumpeter] Eddie Thompkins playing the high ones, and we were standing right in front of the bandstand waiting for this fella. They got to this number he was introduced in and he nearly blew my head off there! Just two white people – the wife and I – amid a sea of black people.' Delighted with their night, the Gonellas fell into bed at six in the morning and, awaking in the afternoon, went out again to hear Abe Lyman's band. But finally fatigue caught up. Returning to the Piccadilly, Nat decided to close his eyes for a nap before setting off again to go on the town. He woke at two the following afternoon on the bed, his trousers still on.

While in New York, another priority for Gonella was to visit Louis Armstrong and he caught up with him at a combined movie and stage-show at the Strand Theatre to promote Louis' latest film *Goin' Places.* On-stage, Armstrong (whose co-star was Bill Robinson) fronted Luis Russell's band and Nat noticed that his idol had put on weight. He was playing as brilliantly as always and greeted his visitor warmly.

Nat had, of course, taken his trumpet on holiday with him. His first opportunity to play came at Nick's Tavern in Greenwich Village, the celebrated base of most of Eddie Condon's early New York activities, run by pianist Nick Rongetti. Bobby Hackett had the band at Nick's and Nat thought he was the closest thing to Bix Beiderbecke he had heard live. The relief band at the club was led by Sidney Bechet and Bechet's power – as well as the skills of drummer

Zutty Singleton – were enthralling to the British visitor. A request to sit in with Hackett's group was granted with impressive results and when, next night, the American developed a gumboil condition and could not front the band, Rongetti invited Gonella to take his place. While he was on the stand, fellow trumpeter Wingy Manone (whose hits Nat had regularly covered in Britain, on Parlophone, over the past four years) came in and a duo set was planned. Bruce Adams – Gonella's later protégé and a close friend – remembers:

> Wingy refused to talk about what they were going to play, and to make matters worse he talked in black slang which made things difficult to understand. Anyhow, the drinks started and, you know, Nat was never a great drinker; two or three scotches at most. Wingy said, 'I got to warm up,' and drank a whole bottle of Scotch, down in one, just before the two of them went on. And Nat blew him off the stage!

Other great American experiences included a visit to the Hotel New Yorker on the night when – amid a host of celebrities – Jimmy Dorsey handed over his band residency to brother Tommy. Gonella travelled to Philadelphia to hear Count Basie's band too, and met or rubbed shoulders with a host of other fellow performers during his visit. Among them were Duke Ellington, Artie Shaw, Chick Webb, Noble Sissle, Claude Hopkins, Teddy Hill, Roy Eldridge, Ben Webster, Dicky Wells, Phil Napoleon, Glenn Miller, Johnny Mercer, Joe Venuti, Red McKenzie, Pee Wee Russell and Billie Holiday. When Nat spotted Fats Waller again in a 52nd Street club, he half-stood to hold out his hand in greeting. Waller ignored him completely, but two hours later returned to Gonella's table and greeted him like a long-lost relation. 'You're a funny bugger!' observed the trumpeter with characteristic bluntness. 'When you first came in you ignored me.' 'I was cold sober,' Waller beamed. 'I never recognise anyone until I've had a drink.'

In another club on the Street, Nat met and befriended clarinettist/bandleader Joe Marsala, who invited his visitor to take part in the now-legendary 'St Regis Jam Sessions', broadcast live to England from the St Regis Hotel, hosted by Alistair Cooke and featuring most of New York's jazz aristocracy. Nat was delighted but, in the event, the broadcast's time was put forward from four to two o'clock in the afternoon. When he arrived, the trumpeter had only the time (and presence of mind) to find a microphone and announce over the air, 'Hello England; this is Nat Gonella,' rather than to play.

Word was spreading around New York about the dynamic trumpeter from England who could easily rival his American counterparts, and offers of work were forthcoming. It was probable that there was plenty of money to be made in the USA and Nat began procedures to file for American citizenship. Mountains of forms and interviews to attend were a natural barrier but the wheels were in motion and Stella Moya loved the fast American lifestyle.

For Nat, his last day in New York proved unforgettable. As he had told his record company, one priority during his visit was to make records and on 20 January he cut four sides with an all-star band assembled by bassist John Kirby and completed by Benny Carter (alto), Buster Bailey (clarinet), Billy Kyle (piano), Brick Fleagle (guitar) and Jack Meisel (drums). 'I'd mentioned to the Decca Record Company that if I'm going over there I'd like to make a record with some American artists,' he told Fairweather. 'So they said, "Well – good idea!" because they had Decca in America as well. So, when we got down there, they'd corresponded and I got introduced to the fellow from the American recording, and they set up a band for me. They had to be New York musicians. And then a fellow came in and he sat down and I said, "Who are you?" And he said, "Well, I'm the leader." I said, "What are you talking about?" He said, "Well, I've got to sit in for you because you're not in the union." So he sat there and they had to pay him full money (thirty-five dollars) because I was doing somebody out of work. He went and sat there; just drank a drop of Scotch with us and enjoyed himself and they gave him the money afterwards. Strong union – especially in those days!'

The session produced high-class jazz; on the recordings Carter's elegant alto and Kyle's pearl-scattering piano lines provide the perfect accompaniment for Gonella's trumpet which rises to its surroundings and even, on one track, 'I Must See Annie Tonight', races along exuberantly slightly ahead of its rhythm section. The records are central to Gonella's discography. As Humphrey Lyttelton says in the sleevenote to the album *Georgia Boy from London*:

> If they fall short of the very best that might have come from this collaboration it's largely due to the Decca company's insistence on currently commercial material. Nevertheless, the sessions produced their fair share of delights, not least of which is the sound of Nat's chirpy Cockney voice, unabashed and with not even a mid-Atlantic tinge, in the midst of Carter, Bailey and Kyle. 'You Must Have Been a Beautiful Baby' opens with one of the best bits of trumpet in the whole set, relaxed yet decisive, in close touch with the beat, and with a singing tone suggestive here of Bunny Berigan. Throughout, Nat asserted his leadership with no apparent excess of awe.

A sense of awe was certainly no part of Gonella's make-up. For Digby Fairweather the outstanding track is 'Just a Kid Named Joe', a lyrically touching medium-tempo ballad about a newsboy, written the year before by the partnership of Mack

David and Jerry Livingston. 'That was a good one, wasn't it, yeah!' Gonella agreed. 'Got to have a little bit of pathos in that, didn't you?'

Nat and Stella spent their last night in New York at the Cotton Club, packed with celebrities, many of them there to say farewell to Abe Lyman who was taking his band to Miami for a season. Among the visitors were: the Andrews Sisters (Patti, Laverne and Maxine), enjoying the success of their first big hit, 'Bei mir bist du schoen'; the Green Sisters, just starting their career; and the Mills Brothers, all enjoying Cab Calloway's band and floorshow. 'Cab couldn't talk to me,' Nat told Sheila Tracy, 'as he wasn't allowed to come across the footlights because all the people on-stage were black and the clientele were white and it was like that in those days.' With Gonella and Moya in the audience was boxer Tommy Farr, who had been beaten a week earlier by Red Burman and was in need of a cheerful evening (when Farr eventually returned to Britain he had lost all five of his bouts). The trumpeter was amused to note that Farr had a bodyguard with him. Such was the state of the sport in America, with both gangsters and gambling involved, that boxers could often earn more money by losing than winning. The Cotton Club was richly populated with boxers that night: Joe Louis and Max Baer were among the visiting stars, and at one point Farr was called out and introduced to the audience. Assuring the audience that he would not try to sing, he nevertheless said that he knew a man who could: a great jazz trumpeter from England called Nat Gonella. 'All Cab Calloway's band fell off their seats nearly,' Gonella told Fairweather. 'And I said, "Well I haven't got no horn." So they all rushed to the front of the stage to lend me their trumpet.' With a strange horn and mouthpiece (no small challenge to a lesser talent), Gonella led Calloway's band into

'Ain't Misbehavin'', receiving ecstatic applause supplemented by the thunder of gavels supplied by the management for enhanced expressions of appreciation on the club tables. After the shouts of 'Encore', he gave out with 'Old Man Mose'. 'You wouldn't expect the band to know that one now, would you?' Nat mused to Fairweather. 'And they played it perfectly.'

Possibly the song was a Calloway special but, either way, Nat walked back to his table a hero. Before the night was over Farr's bodyguard had introduced him to the owner of the Cotton Club, who also happened to be Joe Louis' manager and was reputed to have strong underworld connections. This powerful figure offered Gonella an appearance at the 1939 World's Fair in New York and almost simultaneously he was approached by Abe Lyman with a view to a contract. This was further reassurance that, if his naturalization went through (and the American musicians' union gave its blessing to the arrangement), there would be no shortage of work for Nat in New York and beyond.

Next day, 21 January 1939, Nat and Stella sailed for Britain. As their liner steamed out of New York harbour, the trumpeter looked back at the skyline and wondered how long it might be before he would return to begin a new phase in his career. The rumours of war which were circulating he put out of his mind amid the elation. But soon those rumours would return and quash his American dream for good.

With a week's voyage ahead to ruminate on his experiences and compare them with Britain's musical scene, Nat had time to think about what he had heard and seen and compare it with conditions back home. He concluded that British musicians were sometimes just as capable and creative as Americans but lacked the opportunities (and sometimes publicity) to turn them into stars. America was seen then – much as it is now – as the hotbed of jazz music. He also noted that American musicians enjoyed more relaxed on-stage conditions and were encouraged to play hot music for fun. Sometimes though, their extrovert behaviour was prompted by drink or even drugs, the latter generally unacceptable in British dance band circles.

Nat had momentarily experimented with drugs early in his career with the Lew Stone band. A colleague had produced marijuana in a joint and – thinking that it might improve his performance – Nat tried it. The high it produced during a recording session prompted him to stand three feet from the recording microphone, ignoring the requests of the sound engineer. After one take his hands started to shake, making any attempt to hold the trumpet steady – and therefore to play properly – an impossibility. The episode represented Gonella's one and only experiment with anything stronger than alcohol.

In fact, the trumpeter needed no more than music and a good night to produce a personal high. Bassist Charlie Winter claimed to remember a concert when the power of Nat's solo blowing seemed to carry the trumpeter into another world and, to allow the performance to carry on, Bob Dryden came from behind his drums and slapped his leader's face. Such an action, if taken, was dangerous, posing a threat to the trumpeter's embouchure. But, according to Winter, it refocussed Gonella's attention on the tune at hand, reassuring his disconcerted band, and within seconds they got on with their show.

Once back in England, Nat and the Georgians with Stella Moya embarked on a Moss Empires tour with comedian Vic Oliver (who found radio fame in the *Hi Gang* show hosted by Bebe Daniels and Ben Lyon). In between dates, Nat took every opportunity to visit the races, often with Stella. In March 1939 the *Daily Sketch* featured the singer decked out in the latest fashion for female race-goers: a kidskin coat with matching handbag, and net cap with beaver ear-muffs. The effect, the ecstatic correspondent reported, was sensational.

While the *Daily Sketch* enthused over Moya's racing garb, *Rhythm Magazine* ran an article on the performing idiosyncrasies of top bandleaders. Benny Goodman, the journal reported, always tweaked each end of his bow tie before taking the stage; Tommy Dorsey checked his trombone slide for mobility, and Nat Gonella looked down at the fingers of his outstretched hand while awaiting his entry. Watching Nat performing forty years on, Ron Brown noted that nothing had changed: Gonella still did the same while waiting for his vocal chorus.

In June 1939 Nat was asked to co-judge the All-Britain Dance Band Championships at Blackpool's Winter Gardens. No fewer than thirty-eight good bands competed for the coveted Jack Hylton Cup, won that year by Londoner Billy Lawrence's band. By this time, however, the Georgians were recording less than in previous years, although well-liked sides from the twenty-four titles they recorded in 1939 included 'Hold Tight' and 'Three Little Fishes' (which combined the vocal stylings of Gonella and Moya), as well as 'One O'Clock Jump', 'T'aint What You Do' and 'Boogie Woogie'. Jimmy Messini also featured on 'South of the Border' and 'Deep Purple'.

Although the Georgians presented themselves as a happy-go-lucky outfit, off-stage their music-making was a serious business and every note and word was thoroughly rehearsed. Gonella was a tough taskmaster and expected a 100 per cent commitment from his musicians. This was revealed in a *Melody Maker* article of the time in which reporter Andy Gray sat in on a Georgians rehearsal prior to their tour of

Scandinavia. Everyone including Stella Moya was present, apart from Bruts Gonella who knocked at the door thirty minutes late. Gray's report went into print as a word-for-word account.

'"Where the hell have you been?" yelled the aggrieved leader. "This rehearsal started half an hour ago. You want to come to Scandinavia, don't you?" The scolded younger brother accepted the public tirade, then apologised. "All right!" Nat concluded, "Get your trumpet and get to work!"'

After the rehearsal, Nat spoke to Gray. 'Bruts isn't in the act yet,' he explained, 'but I use him in my radio shows and special tours. He's coming along and I expect he will join the act permanently soon. He isn't going to get any special privileges because he's my brother – I take him on as a trumpeter, not as a relation.' As they left the rehearsal room, the reporter asked Nat, 'What does the band like playing best?' Without hesitation Gonella returned the perfect answer: 'Poker!'

On 15 August 1939 – less than a month before the outbreak of war – Nat Gonella and his Georgians flew off for a tour of Sweden. They had no idea that this was to be their swan-song. The Georgians would be early victims of the hostilities to come.

7

*If I Only Had Wings**

Comprising chiefly one-night stands, the Georgians' Scandinavian tour was initially scheduled to last three weeks. It was their second trip to Sweden, and on their previous visit venues had mostly proved small; once they had travelled all night to discover that their concert was to take place in a schoolhouse. This time the itinerary was more ambitious, including Stockholm and other cities, with detours to Holland for several shows. All the members of the band were looking forward to the tour; in particular Stella Moya, who had been favoured on the Georgians' previous visit by the award of honorary membership of the Swedish musicians' union.

One concert, in Amsterdam, was a royal command performance for Prince Bernhardt, and Gonella, anxious to ensure that everything would be musically immaculate, pleaded with Jimmy Messini to avoid excessive drinking. The guitarist/singer agreed and the first half of the concert proceeded smoothly. During the interval Nat enquired if every-

*Odeon, Nat Gonella with Thore Ehrling, 13.9.1939

thing was alright. His sideman nodded. 'So far so good Nat – but I'm dry, and I've got my big number coming up. I really could use a drink.'

Gonella relented. 'OK, Jimmy. I'll have the waiter put one in the wings for you.'

A glass of schnapps was brought to the guitarist, but unfortunately the waiter had filled it to the brim. To complicate matters, Messini had secretly drunk his customary amount of whisky before the show anyway and, with the schnapps on top, was in possession of enough Dutch courage to drive a windmill. Soon afterwards Messini's big moment arrived. Nat moved to the microphone. 'Your Royal Highness, ladies and gentlemen! Please welcome – to sing the "Donkey Serenade!" – Jimmy Messini!' The Georgians played his introduction; Messini rose from his on-stage seat to take his place at the microphone and fell flat on his face. Nat recovered sufficiently to grab the microphone. 'Your Royal Highness, ladies and gentlemen! It seems that Jimmy has been overcome by nerves, having to sing before such a distinguished audience.' Sympathetic calls echoed around the hall and Messini was carried tenderly off-stage on a stretcher by two ambulancemen, receiving the biggest applause of the night as he made his inert departure.

Apart from such hitches, the tour began smoothly. But war was now imminent. Band wives and girlfriends back in Britain sent frantic cables advising immediate return, but none was received. The Georgians played on happily enough until they arrived in Kristinehamn, Sweden, on 3 September, the day that Britain declared war on Germany. Sea and air connections between Britain and the Continent were immediately suspended, leaving thousands of Britons high and dry. These included a number of prominent entertainers: Will Hay was stranded in Norway and Bobby Howes in France. But feelings in the Georgians ran high as Nat, they claimed, had told them that – in the event of war – a plane was standing by to take them home. Whether this had been the case at one point, it was certainly not so now. Angriest of all were Dryden, Messini, and alto saxophonist Jimmy Williams who had augmented the Georgians for the tour. In a hotel bedroom Dryden continued stirring up Messini and Williams against their leader, suggesting that Gonella would look after Stella and brother Bruts, leaving them stranded abroad. What they did not know was that, through thin bedroom walls, Nat and Stella had heard every word of the outburst. The stage was set for an acrimonious showdown. Nat announced that he, Stella, Bruts and the youthful Harold Hood would stay in Stockholm and find work there until the war's end, or until a safe passage back to England was assured. The rest of the band could make their own plans.

Naturally everyone was anxious to find some way back to England. Pat Smuts and Charlie Winter decided to make a dash for Copenhagen in the hope of finding a boat. But none was leaving for England, so they returned to Malmö to approach the British consul and local police for help. All routes to England – via Bergen, Gothenburg and Esbjerg – were shut; however, a plane was leaving for England on 10 September. After buying tickets, Smuts and Winter had just two pounds left between them. The following Sunday the plane took off on schedule but was diverted to Amsterdam, where the luckless duo found that no flights to London were scheduled as British authorities were denying landing permission. Grasping the hope that a flight might leave next day, they checked in at cheap lodgings for the night and returned to the airport at eight o'clock next morning, penniless. A nine-hour wait without food was rewarded with the dismal news that permission to land in England was still highly unlikely. Smuts and Winter were stranded with no money and nowhere to stay, and went to the British consulate in Amsterdam to explain their predicament. There was still no help to be had. A representative explained that, as they were carrying suitcases and instruments, the two musicians could not be classed as destitute and financial aid was out of the question. Perhaps Smuts might pawn his saxophone?

At this point the duo received a much-needed stroke of luck; an English resident offered a meal and a night's accommodation. Fortified and refreshed, they returned to the airport, once again for an all-day stay with fellow refugees who happened this time to include author H.G. Wells. Eventually the airport authorities came through with an offer: no flights could be guaranteed, but passengers could take a chance on a boat leaving that evening at 10.30 from Rotterdam. Air tickets would be exchanged for boat tickets and free transportation to the port provided. Charlie and Pat jumped at the opportunity, although once on board they were brusquely informed that their tickets did not now include on-board food. Once again a good Samaritan was at hand; a fellow South African who fell into conversation with Smuts and insisted on paying the bill for three meals. At last they arrived back at Gravesend late on the night of 13 September, concerned but relieved to be home.

Smuts and Winter were first to arrive. Bob Dryden, Jimmy Messini and Jimmy Williams chased around Scandinavia trying to use or reclaim the value of their air tickets and travel documents, but all air and shipping routes were closed. An attempt to cross the Channel from Esbjerg was similarly unsuccessful, and the trio returned to the British consulate in Stockholm to be informed that a ship was due to leave Gothenburg for

England on 22 September. The wait of almost two weeks swallowed what little money they had left; Bob Dryden was forced to sell his drum kit and Williams his saxophone. On finally boarding the promised ship, there was trouble over reservations, but fortunately the British consulate resolved the problem before the ship left harbour. Nevertheless they had no idea of their destination; 'somewhere in England' was the only information the shipping company would supply.

No doubt this was in the interests of naval security. A Norwegian ship ahead, taking an alternative outside course, was torpedoed and sunk with all hands. Enemy aircraft harassed their ship, but finally Dryden, Messini and Williams arrived back in England on 26 September after the longest and most worrying twenty-three days of their lives. Minus jobs and instruments, they had nevertheless made it and Bob Dryden declared to a *Melody Maker* reporter, 'We are ready to do whatever we can for our country now that she needs us.'

Perhaps it was as well that Gonella himself was not home to read the paper's headlines (no doubt based on information collected from his aggrieved sidemen). 'Nightmare dash for Georgians,' it proclaimed. 'Stranded in Sweden! Nat Gonella stays over there! Boys left to their own resources! Instruments sold to get back!' The article left little doubt about the ill-feeling between his musicians and Nat himself. While Dryden, Messini and Williams were awaiting their ship, they saw their leader performing in solo cabaret at a big nightclub in Stockholm. Dryden's reaction was brief. 'We didn't speak to him,' he said, 'and he didn't speak to us.'

Gonella seemed to be only marginally concerned about an impending German invasion. He filled in time with gigs wherever he could find them. Sitting on a bandstand with Harold Hood as they discussed their isolated predicament the trumpeter mused 'If I only had wings'! The pianist's response was, 'That sounds like a great title!' Together they composed the cheerful song, first recorded on 13 September 1939 in Stockholm with Thore Ehrling's orchestra for the Odeon label, featuring the three trumpets of Ehrling and the Gonella brothers. ('Sunrise Serenade', a big hit of the time, was the B-side). When the co-composers arrived back in England, 'If I Only Had Wings' was initially shelved as there was another tune of the same title awaiting publication. But, later, it was published by Maurice Music and a stylish version appears on *The Nat Gonella Story*, arranged by Kenny Graham and produced for EMI's Lansdowne series by Denis Preston in 1961.

Nat Gonella's reluctance to escape Sweden may seem hard to understand and Ron Brown found that he was not forthcoming on this episode of his career. Perhaps Nat thought that he did not have any problem with the Germans as he was very popular with German music fans.

In fact, many jazz musicians worked in post-war Germany, finding the cultural acceptance of jazz there greater than in Britain. Germans enjoyed a good time and Hamburg by the 1950s had turned into a jazz stronghold, years before the Beatles arrived there. After rock music changed the face of popular culture in Britain and America, many former stars of the 'trad boom' (including Monty Sunshine and Chris Barber) quickly found a second home on East and West German jazz circuits.

It should also be remembered that Gonella – at only just past thirty – was a big star with a formidable history of success behind him. He possessed a strong nerve, unconquerable courage as a performer and the necessary hint of steel to make hard decisions on his own behalf and in his own interests. He was also a simple, pragmatic man, capable – in all probability –

of holding troubles (or invading forces) at bay until they were knocking at his door.

Not all Germans were Nat Gonella fans, however. Horst Lange, a respected German jazz commentator, supplied a copy of a Nazi information sheet dated 11 October 1938. 'Nat Gonella records,' it read, 'should be ignored; all records played by the nigger-band Nat Gonella are in opposition to the ethic of the German people because of their distorted and squeaking instrumentation.' Despite an apparent national fallibility in the matter of jazz critique, the German war-machine was undeniably moving closer and, travelling in Holland, Gonella found that anti-British propaganda was increasing. More frequently he was asked to play German songs in clubs, but refused to do so. Finally, he became aware that to stay at all was dangerous. It was time to make a run for home.

Nat, Stella, Bruts and Harold left Holland with only days to spare before the Germans marched in. Making their way to the south of France, they joined other stranded Britons waiting with decreasing optimism for the British government to send boats to their rescue. Meanwhile, the Italians bombed Cannes and the situation became desperate. Finally, a rescue ship appeared on the horizon to transport them to Gibraltar and, tired out and traumatised, the quartet boarded the vessel with only the clothes they wore and a trumpet. All their remaining possessions – including six hundred pounds of English money – lay wasted through Sweden, Denmark, Holland and France. Sailing conditions were poor, the boat was crammed with refugees and the eventual sight of Gibraltar was greeted with cheers of relief. The arrivals received a heroes' welcome and hotel accommodation, food and drink, and even cinema visits were provided free of charge. Nat was recognised by troops everywhere and subsequently volunteered for a number of ad hoc concerts. When the tired group of entertainers was due to depart, they had to be smuggled from the garrison, victims of their own popularity.

The conditions of their final flight to freedom resembled a nightmare. Aboard an ancient collier ship, the 670 passengers – most of them living on deck – were soon caked with coal-dust. There was no soap; food and water were rationed, and the weather was terrible. Conditions were so crowded that Nat was forced to sleep under a deck-gun which had been mounted as protection from enemy aircraft. Once, he awoke to hear the gun fired; an enemy submarine had passed under their boat and was now giving chase. The collier was forced to race at twelve knots, rather than its normal maximum of eight; while it shook and shivered, engines groaned under the strain and a deafening rattle announced the presence of steering chains yanking its rudder from side to side. The resultant zigzag course may have helped to steer the ship clear of two torpedoes fired from the submarine and finally the old boat steamed into Liverpool docks to hugs and handshakes. The ordeal was over – and for the Georgians the story was over too.

What happened to them after Nat Gonella? Bob Dryden rejoined the RAF in spring 1940 and played in service bands until demobilization. After that, he worked with bandleader Dave Crook again, and then returned to his old stomping ground, Margate, to play with Frederick Hargreaves before emigrating to Canada in spring 1948. From there he worked on cruise liners with Raymond Lyall, sailing to and from Australia, and died at sea during one such voyage in 1950.

Harold Hood remained a busy professional pianist for thirty-five years after the war. Although details of his career are sketchy, he was certainly back in London's clubland by 1949–50 when he worked with Ronnie Pleydell's band at

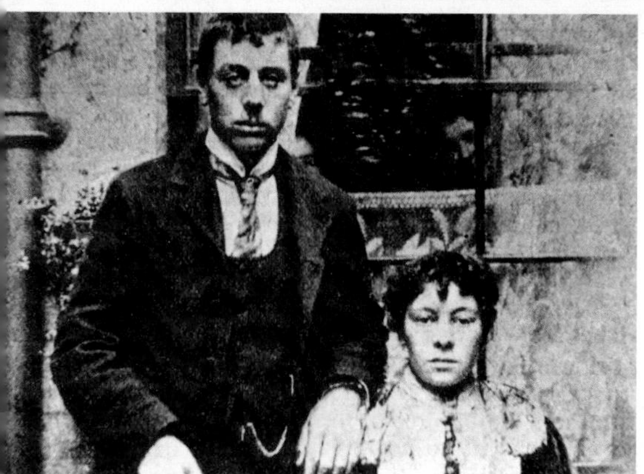

Above: St Mary Guardians School brass band, Islington, c.1917. Nat is sitting to the right of the drums, holding a cornet.

Left: Nat's parents: Richard and Elizabeth Gonella.

Below: Archie Pitt's Busby Boys, c.1926. Nat is fifth from the right; drummer Max Abrams is third from the right.

Above, left to right: Singer Gracie Fields and Nat's first musical employer Archie Pitt; and bandleaders Lew Stone and Roy Fox.

Centre, right: Nat with pianist Garland Wilson in 1933.

Below: The Lew Stone band on the Isle of Man in 1934. Nat was on a variety tour so his brother Bruts stood in for him in the trumpet section.

Above: The Ray Noble band arriving at Rotterdam Airport in 1933. Nat is second from the left, between Tiny Winters and Al Bowlly. Ray Noble and Freddy Gardner kept the British flag flying by wearing plus-fours, while Harry Berly (centre) was prepared for all seasons with raincoat and tennis racket.

Left: Nat and 5-year-old daughter Natalie swing out in 1936.

Below: A beach party at Scheveningen, 1933; *left to right*: Bill Harty and wife, Al Bowlly, Nat (standing), Lew Davis, child, Davis' wife, Freddy Gardner and wife, and Al Bowlly's wife, Marjie.

Above: Nat and his Georgians, complete with clean-cut college image.

Below: A still from the film *Pity the Poor Rich*, 1935, with Pat Smuts (tenor sax), Nat, drummer Bob Dryden, and a hotel commissionaire apparently not amused at the invasion of 'hot' jazz (Butcher films).

Above: Nat and the Georgians embarking on their first tour of Sweden in 1938.

Far left: Nat's younger brother, Bruts.

Centre left: Charlie Winter.

Bottom left: Nat and Stella Moya 'holding that tiger', 1938.

Bottom right: Private Gonella.

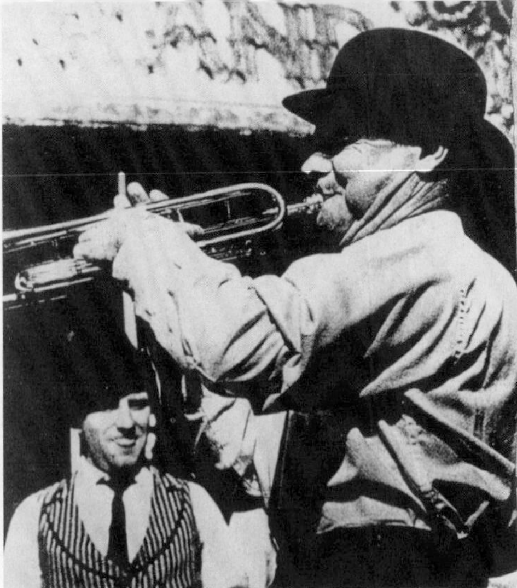

Top left: Charlie Winter, Nat, and Harry Gold at the Gosport Jazz Club in 1987. Charlie and Nat had not met for nearly 50 years.

Top right: Nat impersonates Acker Bilk, complete with bowler hat, watched by Acker himself.

Centre: Nat with his idol. The photo is inscribed: 'To Nat Gonella, My Boy for many years, from Louis Armstrong'.

Bottom: Nat with his wife Dorothy and comedian Max Miller at Great Yarmouth in 1954.

Top: *This is Your Life,* 1960. *Left to right*: Eddie Carroll, Pat Smuts, Alan Duddington, Helen Mack, Lennie Hastings, Nat, Teddy Layton, Dorothy Gonella, Humphrey Lyttelton, Jack Turland, Fred Wood, Bobby Mickleburgh, Lew Stone, Eddie Rogers, George Latimer and Lennie Felix.

Centre: Nat entertains his Dutch fans in 1973 after being crowned Holland's 'King of Jazz' (photo courtesy Wout Meppelink).

Bottom left: Nat singing with American cornettist Warren Vaché and trombonist Roy Williams, June 1990, Concorde Club, Eastleigh (photo by Ian Powell).

Bottom right: Nat with Ron Brown, 1985.

Top: BBC television show at the South Parade Pier, Southsea, 1985. *Left to right*: Beryl Bryden, Humphrey Lyttelton, Nat, Digby Fairweather, and George Turner of Southsea's Savoy Ballroom.

Centre: At the same show, *left to right*: Pete Strange, John Armatage, Digby Fairweather, Humphrey Lyttelton Nat and Paul Sealy (photo courtesy of Malcolm Macdonald).

Bottom: Nat's funeral cortege, led by the Excelsior Marching Band, Gosport, 20 August 1998 (photo *Portsmouth News*).

the Embassy Club in Lower Regent Street. Reedman Roy Willox remembers him well: 'A tremendous player with very good ideas and a wonderful ear. Pleydell would call a tune and he would find the key immediately. But later I never came across him – though I believe he loved to ride horses in his spare time.' Much later, in 1982, Digby Fairweather contacted Hood with a view to joining Tiny Winters and Pat Smuts in a touring package show, *We Remember Nat*. Sadly, he was too ill to take part.

Jimmy Messini teamed with Al Bowlly in early 1940 to form a singing duo billed as 'The Radio Stars with Two Guitars' or 'Two Voices and Guitars in Harmony' to tour the variety circuits. Their recording of 'Only Forever' (a Bing Crosby hit) still sounds charming today. But the partnership was abruptly terminated when Bowlly was killed in his London flat in a bombing raid on 17 April 1941. Sixty years on, Bowlly is a cult figure but his latter-day partner's life is less well documented. At one point, according to researcher Chris Hayes, Messini was held by immigration authorities while trying to enter the USA. In 1988 Doug Wilkins (writing in *Memory Lane*) confirmed, via a fellow researcher in Canada, Lyman Potts, that Messini in later years moved to Montreal where he died in 1969.

Pat Smuts always looked back on the Georgians as the happiest period of his professional life and likened it to being part of a family with Nat Gonella as head. He never denied that Nat had been his inspiration, and continued to assert what was frequently said of the trumpeter: that it would be difficult to find a better friend anywhere. Smuts played with Harry Roy at London's Café Anglais before joining the RAF to play with George Hackford's band, entertaining servicemen all over Europe. From 1945 until late 1955 he worked at the London

Palladium with the Skyrockets, and thereafter freelanced in theatres, nightclubs and hotels for many years. In 1982 he emerged from semi-retirement, still playing strongly, to tour (and later record) with Tiny Winters in Digby Fairweather's New Georgians for early performances of their *We Remember Nat* show. Despite suffering a heart attack later on, Smuts continued playing gigs and raising a new family; he died in London on 10 October 1999 and Fairweather delivered his eulogy.

The indomitable Charlie Winter joined the RAF as a direction-finder, although he also found time to form a small band, the 'RAF Hebridean Band', for troop concerts, and later toured Britain, playing in aerodromes and hospitals. During the conflict a block of flats where he was staying was destroyed by bombing; Winter was pulled from the wreckage six hours later, the only survivor, and taken to a casualty station, where he met his future wife, Irene. After the war he toured variety theatres throughout Britain with Younkman's Czardas Band, as a member of which he was required to don Gypsy costume for each performance. Younkman, who was Latvian, offered family entertainment in every sense; his wife Ludmilla and their two daughters played violins in the ensemble as well as providing a stylish line in Gypsy dancing. Another of Winter's engagements was with Leslie 'Jiver' Hutchinson but he eventually left Hutchinson's band depressed by the fact that, while it was easy for him to find digs on tour, his unfortunate colleagues who were all black were regularly refused accommodation by prejudiced landladies. After an injury in a motorcycle crash in 1951, Winter resumed work with George Crow in 1952 but gave up the bass after sustaining an injury to his hand. Thereafter, he worked for the Shell Oil Company until moving to Australia in 1972, but still came back to Britain for reunions with Nat Gonella.

8

*Bugle Call Rag**

Back in England, the early days of the war were a time for Gonella to pick up the threads of his life. Swing was now king, and big bands were all the rage. But in Britain young musicians were quickly called up and many more, in those patriotic years, enlisted voluntarily to fight for king and country. Several top orchestras were already struggling to maintain their line-up.

In these conditions, Gonella's first thirteen-piece big band, the New Georgians, took to the bandstand. Its line-up comprised Jack Wallace, Cyril Oughton and Nat (trumpets); 'Miff' King (trombone); Jock Middleton, Jack Bonser, Joe Moore and Micky Seidman (reeds); Norman Stenfalt (piano); Roy Dexter (guitar and vocals); Will Hemmings (bass), and Johnny Rowlands (drums), plus Stella Moya. Its repertoire from 1940–41 consisted of a wide range of material chosen principally – as with most of Gonella's output – for commercial appeal. Proven big band or swing hits ('Tuxedo Junction', 'In the Mood') were joined by Gonella specialities ('Oh! Mo'nah',

*Parlophone, Nat Gonella and his Georgians, 7.10.1936

'The Sheik of Araby', 'Georgia on My Mind'), novelty specialities ('Murder!' 'The Hut Sut Song') and popular standards ('Stardust', 'Time on My Hands'). Stella Moya recorded a dozen titles with the band while guitarist Roy Dexter's rich and pleasant voice graced six more. In all, the band recorded seventy sides.

Gonella's aim, on record as well as off, was to cheer factory workers and servicemen as well as beleaguered Britons running to air-raid shelters or sleeping rough in Underground stations. And he could seldom resist a comedy number such as 'South with the Border!' or the even more naughty 'The Man Who Comes Around'. 'I did enjoy the big band for a while, yeah!' he told Digby Fairweather. 'I used to listen to a lot of Harry James and such people and they used to blow over the top of the brass section, didn't they? I wanted to do that – and when I knew I could do it, I thought it was great. It was terrible really, but I enjoyed it.'

There is an interesting story relating to Nat's recordings of 'At the Woodchopper's Ball' and 'In the Mood', cut on 30 October 1940. Although England and Germany were at war, the record – remarkably – was pressed in Berlin for export to Denmark on the HMV label. The original Columbia pressing probably reached Germany via Sweden in 1941 or 1942, and was subbed at the Electrola Works in Berlin. In fact thousands of records were pressed in Germany for export to occupied or neutral countries right up to autumn 1944. Even in war, business is business!

The New Georgians were immediately in demand for concerts countrywide, and posters proclaiming their appearances announced the coming of 'Mr and Mrs Swing'; Nat and Stella had married at Hendon, north London, in the summer of 1940. In the early years of the war the trumpeter regularly played troop concerts, often involving long distances and poor conditions and one such show – in this case near to his Edgware home – stood out in his mind. Although he owned two cars – a Hudson Terraplane and an Opel shooting brake – Gonella rode a motorcycle for short distances in the interests of fuel economy. After his appearance as soloist at an army camp a sergeant offered to drive his star guest home in an army truck with his motorbike on the back. A short way into the journey the passengers discovered that the rear of the truck was on fire; petrol had trickled from Gonella's bike and ignited. Rushing to the vehicle's rear, the soldiers pulled it away and Gonella, finding everything intact, rode away, leaving the troops to put out the blaze.

On 12 July 1941 he guested on a record date for Columbia with youthful trumpeter Johnny Claes and his Claepigeons band featuring, among others, Harry Hayes (alto), Aubrey Frank (tenor), Tommy Pollard (piano), Ivor Mairants (guitar), Charlie Short (bass) and Carlo Krahmer (drums). The record coupled 'Stompin' at the Savoy' with 'How Am I to Know', for which a stylish vocal was supplied by the young Benny Lee. Claes, a Gonella protégé, had come to Britain from Belgium in March 1940. The two became great friends and subsequently, without Nat, Claes recorded eight more sides (including Gonella's old hit 'I Heard'); four of them in October 1941, four more in January 1942. But his career did not stand the test of time. Claes started an export and import company (based in Belgium) after the war and later gave up the trumpet to make his mark as a professional racing driver. He died early from cancer back in his home country in 1956.

In July 1941 the New Georgians began a five-week residency at Glasgow's renowned Green's Playhouse, one of Britain's most prestigious dance halls. But it was while they were completing their term that Gonella was called up for military service.

The turnover in the New Georgians had already been damaging. By this time, as a result of call-up, only two members of the original band remained from the previous year, but to draft a major and high-profile entertainer like Nat Gonella was something else again. In the London *Evening News*, critic Jack Robertson argued the futility of putting celebrities like Gonella into uniform. They would be better employed in raising the spirits of the masses, Robertson claimed, than in digging trenches. And Gonella's regular twenty-five pounds a week in tax provided funds for the War Department and was good reason for exemption. The trumpeter himself was philosophical on the matter. 'Well,' he reflected, 'if I have to go it's nice to think that it's from Green's, the best play-date in the country!' Robertson's column noted that Stella Moya would continue to lead the band during her husband's absence, and a later piece in the *Evening News* described Stella as one of the few women to lead a top-line West End band in London; a small piece of geographic licence as at the time the New Georgians were playing at the Empress, Brixton.

Nat's own description of his interview for the army, as told to Ron Brown, reads like a comedy script:

Officer: 'What are you?'
Gonella: 'I'm a musician.'
Officer: 'Any trade?'
Gonella: 'No sir!'
Officer: 'Well, you're not much good to the army, are you?'
Gonella: 'No sir!'
Officer: 'Well, what's your name?'
Gonella: 'Gonella, sir!'
Officer: 'Ah I see! Italian eh!'

After this simple exchange, Gonella was assigned as a private to the Pioneer Corps, a branch of the army often saddled with the most disagreeable and dirty work. His income dropped from around one hundred and fifty pounds a week to seventeen shillings and sixpence, a total which fell to ten shillings after 'stoppages'. This was belittling enough, but the new recruit was set to the task of digging latrine trenches. Fortunately, by October 1941 he was already leading a small band of musicians in khaki at Belle Vue barracks for troop shows and regimental dances.

Shortly afterwards came another positive development: an entertainment unit of former professional performers drawn from army bases all over Britain was assembled to provide shows at military camps in remote areas. Officially titled 'The Central Pool of Artistes', the unit soon became better known as 'Stars in Battledress'. On the basis of the reputation that Private Gonella was establishing at Belle Vue, he was selected as one of the founding (and later near-legendary) team of entertainers based at the Royal Ordnance Depot, Greenford, Middlesex. He found himself in good company: comedian Charlie Chester, bandleaders George Melachrino and Sid Millward, juggler and unicyclist Boy Foy and actor Stan Hall were fellow recruits. Hall remembers: 'At Greenford life was a bit primitive with quarters in a freezing cold Nissen hut.' And, as a signal reminder to the young entertainers, they were ordered on parade every morning with other recruits at the depot, before retiring to a building known as 'Hut 13' for rehearsals.

The 'Central Pool' formed a motley group on parade. Stan Hall remembers that 'Nat Gonella always arrived in suede shoes and drove a big car which he parked just at the end of the parade ground.' He was not noted for punctuality, though

Charlie Chester observed that parades never seemed to begin until Gonella arrived, usually in his car! 'Some marvellous performers,' Chester remembered, 'but their soldiering wasn't too hot. I mean, could you imagine Terry-Thomas bayoneting anybody? Nat Gonella – a wonderful trumpet player – but he couldn't take an order if you gave him one!' The one thing Private Gonella did take seriously, of course, was music. Whether playing to troops in a NAAFI canteen or a village hall, or even from the back of a lorry in the middle of a field, he consistently played with the same power and commitment as if he were on-stage at the London Palladium. From time to time, too, he would take a night off to visit the Squadronaires as they toured in concert and drink with a good friend, lead trumpeter Tommy McQuater.

As well as doing live appearances, Nat recorded special radio shows for the War Office which were relayed to troops overseas. Meanwhile, at home, Stella Moya struggled to keep the depleted New Georgians together. When leave allowed, Nat was able to join them for concerts around the country. But, although army life had considerably modified his lifestyle and earnings, he was beginning to adjust to it. Until, that is, quite unexpectedly, he was posted abroad. Neither Nat nor his fellow performers could make sense of the decision, and the trumpeter's destination was initially kept secret. He joined troops on a packed ship, to be kitted out with drill shorts and shirts, in preparation – so it was ultimately revealed – for a landing in North Africa. The heat, flies and sand all contributed to the reluctant private's depression. Gonella hated the army and again he was lodged in the Pioneer Corps which was landed with the most unenviable dirty work.

Now though, good luck took a hand. Camped some twenty miles from Nat's unit was the Band of the Royal Tank

Regiment and, on hearing that he was posted nearby, its members invited the star to join them for a performance as guest artist. He accepted the invitation with relief and – following a highly successful troop concert – was transferred immediately to the Tank Regiment for musical purposes. With them, Gonella would travel all over North Africa, as well as into Sicily and Italy.

In the early days of September 1943, allied forces crossed the Straits of Messina and, as they were about to go into battle, a company of Canadian soldiers was entertained by the trumpeter and his new colleagues in a field, surrounded by tents, lorries and armoured vehicles. The night of music passed with sing-songs and plenty of beer and wine. Next morning the Canadians moved off to battle and, as more than thirty-five trucks packed with troops pulled out of camp, Nat Gonella, deeply moved, stood at the gate blowing each vehicle a farewell fanfare.

One of his happier encounters ensued while the regiment was camped near Naples. Dozing in his tent one afternoon, he was abruptly woken: 'Private Gonella! Get on your feet and get fell in outside!' Jumping from his bunk, and scrabbling for belt and beret, the trumpeter took a moment to recognise the face behind the fortissimo command. It was Eddie Carroll, his one-time piano colleague in Lew Stone's orchestra, and now a staff-sergeant in the Royal Army Ordinance Corps. Soon the friends were happily recalling old times; Carroll had led his own bands before the war, including a 1936 spell as musical director for the *Queen Mary*. He continued to lead and play solo in Britain as well as Italy and India after the war and would carry on a career until 1967 when ill-health forced his retirement; he died in 1969.

Although Nat was not to know at the time, his voice and

trumpet were sometimes heard in the desert even when he was nowhere near. Arthur Roberts, an old soldier and desert campaigner, was stationed in 1944 in a North African desert outpost where the only entertainment for soldiers was a cinema four miles away. The walk back to camp after the show through the pitch black of a desert night presented a problem. But a corporal at the camp solved it by playing Gonella's record of 'Stardust' over the loudspeakers of the camp's public-address system to guide troops home.

After their concerts in the Italian campaign, the Tank Regiment band was ordered back to England and Nat was allowed two weeks' leave. Almost immediately, however, his stomach began to trouble him and the trumpeter reported sick. He had developed a duodenal ulcer; which in turn would lead to his departure from the army. He handed in his uniform just days before the Tank Regiment band left for France following the first invasion landings.

Back in civilian life, Gonella contemplated his future. Although pleased to be home and out of uniform, he was also aware that Stella's welcome had been less warm than expected and that his wife of more than three years was now making every available excuse to leave the house. With suspicions growing daily, Nat decided to follow her on one of her nightly excursions. Stella made her way to an Underground station and down an escalator. By dropping behind as he followed, Gonella reached the platform in time to find her locked in a passionate embrace with an American Air Force officer. He hesitated for a moment to decide on his next move, then weighed up the situation realistically. The invading officer was over six feet tall, while he was only five foot three. Logically, and resigned to the situation, he turned and took the escalator back up to the station exit.

Adolf Hitler, Nat Gonella mused, had plenty to answer for. The war with Germany had destroyed his career, broken up his bill-topping band and taken away his American dream. His military service had cost him approximately sixteen thousand pounds in lost earnings. And now it had cost him his marriage, too.

9

*Watcha Gonna Do When There Ain't No Swing?**

With his marriage a thing of the past, Nat Gonella wasted no time moping. He had money saved from the pre-war years and went about spending it as he pleased. 'I suppose,' he said later, 'I became something of a playboy, with the birds and booze, nightclubs and gambling. For me it was easy come, easy go.' But, as his bank balance dwindled and the life of a playboy lost its appeal, putting a band together became not only desirable but a necessity. 'Somebody talked to me about forming a big band,' he said, 'and I did it in Southampton.'

Once his band was assembled, again (as Nat Gonella and his Georgians), Nat took it to Holland under the auspices of impresario Jack Hylton. In an otherwise dismal period, this was a source of personal satisfaction to the trumpeter; he had been one of the last musicians to leave Holland when war broke out and was now one of the first to return. The band comprised: Monty Montgomery, Bruts Gonella and Fred Dinning (trumpets); Frank Osbourne (trombone); Jack Forbes,

*Parlophone, Nat Gonella and his Georgians, 21.4.37

Ken Lumb, Dennis Cracknell and Chris Curtis (reeds); Eddie Farrow (piano); Bill Haines (bass) and the young legend-to-be Phil Seamen (drums). Vocals were shared between the leader and Helen Mack. Nat enjoyed fronting the band. 'There were five brass and I used to do the Harry James thing, then sing a few blues and blow my brains out over the top of the brass section. The gig venues used to be packed with Americans – so much so that, when they eventually left England and went home, the original clientele there wouldn't go in any more. They couldn't go in while the Americans were in there, so they got the needle. You can imagine, can't you?'

Nat was pleased to be working with his brother again. Bruts had served in the Royal Marines band corps but his career – and life – had almost come to an end in 1942 when his ship, H.M.S. *Glasgow*, was torpedoed. The vessel limped into New York and remained there for six months undergoing a refit – a heaven-sent opportunity for Bruts who, as a uniformed officer, was allowed into theatres, shows and clubs free of charge. One night he went to see Tommy Dorsey's orchestra and during the interval went backstage to introduce himself as the brother of Nat Gonella. On discovering that Bruts had his mouthpiece with him, Dorsey lent him a trumpet and invited him to sit in. The version of 'I Can't Give You Anything but Love' that followed earned Bruts a rousing hand. The same night also saw the debut of a skinny, tense young singer with Dorsey's band: Frank Sinatra. On one other night Bruts sat in with the Benny Goodman band to play 'I Found a New Baby'.

The post-war Georgians did not enjoy the recording opportunities of Gonella's earlier bands but nevertheless produced a handful of sides for Decca. These included four from 20 July 1945: 'Ma-Ma', 'Gnat Jump' (a Gonella original), 'Let Him Go Let Him Tarry' and 'Thanks for the Boogie Ride' – as well as

'One Meat Ball' (with vocals by Nat and Helen Mack), 'Put the Blame on Mame' and 'Shoo Fly Pie (and Apple Pan Dowdy)' from 1946. One year later he also re-recorded 'Put the Blame on Mame' (backed with 'Five Minutes More') on a reunion recording session in Sweden with Thore Ehrling's orchestra. This would be his last recording session for ten years.

Monty Montgomery played lead trumpet with the Georgians and fondly recalled his time with the orchestra to Digby Fairweather. 'Yes, Phil [Seamen] and I worked for Nat and he was the greatest, the best. About once a week he would sack Phil or myself for cheek or something; then the next day he would take us back again. That sound of his was enormous. We played Green's in Glasgow and there would be thousands of dancers on the ballroom floor, but you could go to the back of the hall and still hear Nat as clear as a bell. Yes, a marvellous man to work for, and a magnificent jazz musician.'

Joyce Stone told Fairweather how Helen Mack joined Gonella's band and how his new Southampton residency had come about. 'During the war, Lew [Stone] was playing at the Court Royal Hotel in Southampton, run by a Mr Lloyd; we were there from January 1944 till after VE Day. Dorothy [later Nat's wife] and two other girls – all red-heads – used to come in every night. They'd all sit together and dance with the Americans, for whom we were playing almost exclusively – I'd say thirty Americans to every British sailor. They were coming off the LST [landing ship tank] boats. Well, the three red-heads got to know little Helen Mack, who was our singer – she's out in San Francisco now, married to a very nice ophthalmic surgeon – and when we left Southampton to go to the Embassy Club in Bond Street, Nat followed us into the Southampton hotel. We couldn't take Helen, who was only fourteen, to the Embassy Club, so we had to leave her behind and we handed her over to Nat and she worked with him for quite a time. Then he left after a few weeks. But that's where he met Dorothy, of course.'

Bassist Jack Fallon remembers: 'Nat told me a very funny story about when he was down at Southampton. A great big guy was causing a lot of trouble so Nat walked up and whacked him. And this guy knocked poor Nat flying! He said there was no point in attacking this guy – and no point in getting up, either.'

Helen Mack was full of praise for Nat Gonella as a bandleader. On one particular concert at Rhyl, when the band's pianist failed to arrive, she offered to fill in for him and, although she thought her own playing was 'lousy', found that at the week's end Gonella had paid her extra for her efforts.

Occasional disasters struck, however. In 1946 Nat employed a male vocalist destined to hit the headlines for quite the wrong reasons. He was paid three pounds and ten shillings a week (a good wage for the period), but supplemented his income privately as a burglar. He was arrested, one night after the Georgians had played the Savoy Ballroom in Southsea, for breaking into two houses in the area to steal various items, including a £150 diamond ring. When brought up before the magistrates it transpired that his police record included cases of assault, indecent assault, forging a Post Office savings book and several thefts; in addition he was a deserter from the Royal Marines. Gonella was first to admit that this was not the kind of record the Georgians favoured and the vocalist's next residency involved a one year engagement at one of His Majesty's prisons.

It was in May 1946 at the Court Royal Hotel that Helen Mack introduced Nat to his third and last wife, Dorothy. According to Dorothy, who was sitting with a group of girlfriends, Nat's opening gambit was abrupt. 'Right!' he said. 'Who's going to sleep with me?' For a high-profile star such a conversational gambit was perhaps not exceptional (nor necessarily impractical), but Dorothy ignored it and was not initially enamoured, finding Nat to be somewhat irritable. Helen tactfully explained that Nat's stomach ulcers were the cause; Dorothy felt sorry for him and made a special trip to a New Forest farm for new-laid eggs – a definite luxury in ration-bound, post-war Britain. Romance followed and for Nat Gonella it was third time lucky. Natalie Wilson said, 'He and Dorothy finally decided to make a go of it after several years.' They would remain together for nearly fifty years until her death in 1995.

In Britain musical fashions were changing. Headlines in the *Melody Maker* and other trade papers were regularly devoted, on the one hand, to the American bebop revolution of Charlie Parker and Dizzy Gillespie and, on the other, to the classic jazz revival spearheaded in Britain by George Webb's Dixielanders and, soon after, Humphrey Lyttelton. The musical hiatus caused by six years of war had created revolutions in musical thought and a need to find new heroes. This was a problem that Gonella would have to try to conquer. But, although he did so very successfully by and large, he suffered in the same way that hundreds of pre-war rhythm stylists (often with fine technique and talent) did too. Simply, they were forgotten. A new generation of players had no wish – for the moment – to return to the polyglot mix of comedy, sentiment and entertainment that pre-war big bands had mixed with their jazz. The formula seemed old, stuffy and unfocussed, and had been blown away by the realities of war.

Gonella responded to these postwar challenges in various

ways. As a solo performer he continued to draw crowds and appeared with small bands of his own. In June 1946 he played a week's residency in Southend on Sea doubling at the Gliderdrome and the Kursaal Ballroom, attracting fans from London who travelled to see their idol. One-time singer and lifelong jazzlover Gladys Baldwin remembers the season: 'I used to sing in juvenile shows for the troops at Southend Garrison before I was evacuated and used to see Nat, playing with a pickup band of Army musicians including Geraldo's bassist and some of Billy Ternent's sidemen. And I sang with him too. The last time I sang with Nat was at the Kursaal and he had a seven or eight-piece band including Dill Jones, who was stationed at the end of Southend Pier; so that was very handy.'

During this period Nat also formed a comedy group (others like Dr Crock and His Crackpots, Sid Millward's Nitwits and Freddie Mirfield's Garbage Men, all inspired by Spike Jones and his American contemporaries, were similarly major attractions on the halls) and later formed a bebop group, including such young stars as Johnny Rogers (alto), Kenny Graham (tenor), Roy Plummer (guitar), Lennie Bush (bass) and Phil Seamen (drums). While the music initially sounded strange to Gonella, his widely quoted dismissal of the genre as 'gas-oven music' (actually his wife's term) is possibly an over-simplification. In a 1962 'In My Opinion' feature for *Jazz Journal*, something of the duality of Gonella's feelings still came across. Reviewing 'The Meetin'' (1960) by Oliver Nelson's sextet, he said:

> That's a refreshing sound after all that trad stuff. It's not too far out, being rather the equivalent of what I'd call modern-swing style. That far-out stuff [possibly he meant the free jazz of radicals like Ornette Coleman, which had achieved notoriety in the

jazz press] has caused more people to put their heads in gas ovens than anything else I know. These modernists are technically first-class but playing so much in the minor as they do is apt to make them sound morbid and depressed... I have several records of Miles Davis which I bought to listen to, but I daren't play them at home. My missus calls them gas-oven music. One of the troubles of much of this modern jazz is that it goes on much too long, and the musicians haven't all that much to say. Keep it short and it can be attractive in small doses.

Despite his reservations, Gonella was clearly capable of encompassing much of the new music's creative demands. And – as with players like Harry James in the USA – the technical demands of the music would have presented him with few problems in trumpet terms, even if the harmonic challenges of the music were momentarily demanding. He may also have changed his views somewhat with the passage of years. 'Nat was a fantastic player,' Lennie Bush told Sheila Tracy for *Talking Swing*. 'Kenny Graham did a bit of writing and he got him interested in bebop and we would do things like "Groovin' High". Nowadays he denies he ever liked bebop, calls it rubbish, but he was mad about it at the time and we used to play a lot of bebop tunes.' Tapes exist of Gonella playing in variety with a quintet including pianist Denny Termer, guitarist Roy Plummer and bassist Bush, and he sounds completely at home in a more contemporary setting.

Nevertheless, by 1962, Gonella had returned comprehensively to his Armstrong roots. Just as Louis was to reply, 'What's that?' when interviewer Ed Murrow asked him 'What's bop?' (in the 1956 documentary *Satchmo the Great*), so his British disciple was to deny – if not thrice – any interest in modern jazz:

I had the first modern band in the country two years before any-

> one else and I used to drive myself mad trying to blow that stuff. I used to listen to those old bop records and we used to churn it out, but it wasn't any use. I got so nervy I used to go to bed every night with a headache. Terrible, man – I cut it out!

Besides the musical challenges of playing an entirely new form of jazz, Gonella was facing two unavoidable problems in the postwar years. The first was that bebop belonged to a new generation of British players who, with their fans, saw Nat as unavoidably out of fashion, however good a musician he remained. The second was that dance hall proprietors were as reserved about bebop as they had been about swing ten years previously. 'This is bebop; it's the new music,' Nat would explain, to receive the blunt answer from employers, 'Well take it away and don't bring it back!' Nevertheless, his band worked reasonably regularly and, as Lennie Bush remembers: 'We toured one-night stands and every now and again a week in variety with his New Georgians. On the variety dates it was a quintet with Roy Plummer, who went to Australia, and Denny Termer. There was a singer as well: Helen Mack. We used to do all these funny tunes!'

Surrounded by young musicians – many of them exploring bebop's drug culture – Nat wanted no part of the action. 'A couple of my band smoked at one time when we started the modern music and I changed my band,' he told Sheila Tracy. 'They tried to get the girl vocalist smoking it as well and I went in one night and there they were with a bowl and long pipes like the Chinese. "You're only getting half a chorus tonight, what do you want to start getting high for?" It was a dance and we played arrangements so half a chorus was about the most we did.' He also spoke about the brilliant and tragic drummer Phil Seamen, who had his first job with Gonella and, like Bush, adored Nat. 'I knew his mother and father very well.

He hadn't ever had a drink until he'd been with me for just over a year and it was his birthday and somebody enticed him to have half a bottle of beer and he got high on that, walked backwards and fell on his drums. From that moment on he started drinking and eventually got into drugs. Several of my musicians were like that, which was a shame, but you couldn't stop them.'

One more setback for Gonella after the war was his rejection for broadcasting by the BBC. A former Australian bandleader, Jim Davidson, was hired to take charge of the BBC's variety department and when Gonella applied for band broadcasts he was curtly informed that an audition was required. Davidson made it clear that he had not heard of Nat Gonella and was searching for a Harry James soundalike. Politely but firmly Nat made it clear that not only was he a star but that he played in his own style; nevertheless, he duly assembled a backing group and performed for Davidson and a panel of six producers. For his trouble he was treated to the dismissive response, 'We'll let you know.' After twenty years of broadcasting as a distinguished radio star, Britain's hero of a few years before was summarily rejected by the BBC.

One day in Archer Street Nat met his old friend Roy Dexter, who was now playing double bass. Dexter was in trouble, Nat recalled to Digby Fairweather: 'He was in a double act with a trumpet player. The trumpeter died suddenly and I said, "Well, I'm not doing a lot of work and he's gone upstairs so I'll deputise for him! So I learned the act."' This involved another audition, this time at a Butlin's hotel near Brighton, and for it Gonella and Dexter prepared several numbers, including 'Big Noise from Winnetka' for which Nat played drumsticks on the strings of Dexter's bass. Once again, however, they faced rejection.

Salvation arrived via Hal Monty's theatrical agency which had been asked to provide turns for American bases on the Continent. Gonella and Dexter left for Paris and booked in at a modest hotel. The next day they contacted Monty's intermediary, Ted Easton, who was entertainments officer for US forces in France and had a ten-day datesheet ready for the duo. For their first engagement they travelled in Easton's new car, but the double bass was then deemed anti-social cargo in his gleaming automobile and alternative transportation had to be arranged. Rail seemed an obvious choice but, for one appearance some way from Paris, they were stopped by a porter who would not let Dexter's bass on the train. Amid argument and angry gesticulating the train moved off and the duo hurried back to the hotel to consult railway timetables with Ted Easton. An express train would get them there on time, so all three men returned to the station and, while Easton distracted the porter, Gonella and Dexter humped the bass into a carriage. Arriving at their destination, they discovered that Hal Monty had sold them as a fifty- minute act. They had prepared only a quarter of an hour's material but with Nat's trumpet and fast thinking they somehow filled the slot. Nevertheless, the whole ten-day sojourn was depressing to Gonella, whose catalogue of post-war failures seemed to be turning out as dismally as his pre-war career had been triumphant. The only dividend in future years would come from his contact with Ted Easton, a musician who would play a big part in Gonella's later career.

Gonella and Dexter spent the summer of 1949 playing on the Isle of Wight, doubling on Sandown Pier and the Sandringham Hotel as a trio with drummer Les Jessop. Then, after a winter of touring mainland clubs, Gonella bid his partner goodbye and went into solo cabaret in summer 1950 for a season as musical director at the Coronation Holiday Camp, Hayling Island, near Portsmouth. Most nights he played in Ye Olde Barn, an on-camp nightclub, accompanied by piano and drums, and in the Coronation Ballroom opposite clarinettist Johnny Lyne's band. On Sunday his band was increased to a nine-piece while on Thursdays he sat in with the Stan Matthews Quartet, a popular group in the Portsmouth area. Dorothy and their Alsatian Georgia – every Gonella dog had the name – were able to join him for a pleasant and steady stay (which at least involved regular playing). And when the season was over Nat moved west to Southampton to direct a five-piece band in a restaurant attached to the Palm Court Sports Stadium. This was used for both greyhound and speedway racing and one night, for a bet, Nat rode pillion on the back of a motorcycle taking the bends at 35 m.p.h. while he clung on with one hand, playing trumpet with the other. The bet was hard won as cinders flew up from the track into his face as well as the bell of his horn! Playing in a restaurant adjoining a stadium also allowed the trumpeter to combine two passions: while on the bandstand he could signal through the window to a nearby friend to place bets on dogs he fancied.

In this period he also played as star soloist on music-hall bills around London and the South of England. 'It would have been in the late 1940s,' bassist/bandleader Ron Russell remembers, 'and I saw him at Lewisham Hippodrome. You used to pay one shilling to go and sit up in the gods; the second balcony, on the bench seats. Nat came on to play with the pit band and I'll never forget, he started "Georgia" and made a muck-up of the opening. But he was quite natural, no panic. Just laughed and said, "We'll start that again, then." Which he did.'

Traditional jazz rapidly gained in popularity as the 1950s progressed; a trend that would culminate in the hugely successful 'trad boom' of the pre-Beatles 1960s, starring Acker Bilk, Kenny Ball, Chris Barber and their hit-parading contemporaries. Nat Gonella, however, moved in different circles and his background in variety prompted him to gravitate naturally back to older contemporaries for appearances on stage and radio. Among the latter (apparently the BBC had forgotten their audition) was a weekly appearance on comedian Leon Cortez' *'Appy 'Arf 'Our*. Cortez was at that time popular for his 'Cockney Professor' routine as well as his 'Cockney Costers Band', and his partner Doreen Harris was equally well-known as singer and as Cortez' comedy foil. Londoner Nat fitted the show's concept to perfection and before his weekly solo would exchange scripted cross-talk with his partners. In one sketch Harris supposedly produced a telegram from a listener which Gonella read out loud: 'Dear Mr Gonella: when you sing, your voice swells to high heaven!' Cortez riposted: 'That's not "swells". It's "smells!"' Subsequently he would introduce the trumpeter: 'And now mates, it has been said that Nat Gonella is the world's finest trumpet player. Now here's the man who said it – Nat Gonella!' The solo that followed, accompanied by large studio orchestra and sometimes a vocal group too, included showcases such as 'St. Louis Blues' and 'Ciribiribin'– ironically, the kind of material requested by the BBC's Jim Davidson a few years before.

Cortez' show toured in variety, too, although the circuit – like vaudeville in the USA – was being hit by the 'girlie shows'. These were variety's answer to the invasion by television of Britain's households, following the Coronation of 1953. For some time, smaller theatres (Collins Music Hall on Islington Green or Camden Town's Bedford Theatre) hung on with shows such as *Nudes of the World* or *Strip Strip Hooray!* often featuring Phyllis Dixey, 'Jane' of the *Daily Mirror* (real name

Christabel Leighton-Porter), Rosemarie Andree and Ramena. By the end of the decade, strip clubs had replaced 'girlie shows' and variety shows had transferred to the small screen.

Gonella witnessed the death-throes of variety halls in sympathetic and high-profile company by touring for three years with a legendary British comedian, Max Miller. The 'Cheeky Chappie', as he was known, could still draw good audiences at Britain's remaining theatres in the mid-1950s, and Gonella's name was a desirable bonus on the bill. Their supporting acts included Margaret and Billy West, Clarkson and Leslie and high-wire walker 'Georgette'. The two entertainers got on well both on- and off-stage, though Miller lived up to his reputation as a tightwad. He would make a grand entrance in a Rolls-Royce to the town hosting his theatrical presence for a week's run (for which the local press were notified). Then, Gonella would be expected to drive Miller to appearances, turning the trumpeter into an unpaid chauffeur.

Miller's catch-phrase, 'Now there's a funny thing,' originated from his stage-gag: 'Now 'ere's a funny thing. I went home to the wife last night. Now there's a funny thing!' One night, the tables were turned. Miller was playing at Portsmouth's Theatre Royal and afterwards ran for the station, arriving just in time to view the last train pulling out. A nearby porter riposted: 'Now there's a funny thing!' Miller's reply was unprintable.

During an engagement at Brighton Hippodrome in 1954, the two stars were drinking in the theatre bar when a road labourer, dressed in rough-cord trousers tied at the knees with string, joined them uninvited. Thrusting an empty glass under the man's nose, Miller requested 'Gin!' and, once the unwanted visitor had hailed the barman, barked the order: 'Make it a double!' Then he took the glass and turned his back on the intruder. Nat left to go on-stage and when he got back saw the same routine repeated, word for word.

Miller was an excellent golfer and though Gonella played less well he often accompanied the comedian to local courses to form foursomes with unsuspecting club members, delighted to be playing with celebrities. A bet on the side would be arranged to make the match more interesting, and thereafter Miller would raise his game. Nat noted that the comedian made plenty of money with the trick, no doubt to his opponents' surprise and consternation.

Like Jack Benny and Sir Harry Lauder, Miller thrived on a reputation for meanness but could also display generosity. He was especially charitable to blind people, a result of three days of sightlessness that he had suffered himself during action in the First World War. During the Second World War he loaned his Ovingdean mansion to St Dunstan's as an annex to the main blind home, and was generous to blind performers, including his own pianist, Alfred Thripp, who shared support billing with Gonella on theatre appearances. However, he also had a reputation for not suffering fools gladly. Fortunately, he liked both Nat and Dorothy Gonella and one Christmas a van arrived at their Edgware home to deliver a fully decorated Christmas tree laden with parcels, a gift from the comedian. 'He wasn't mean,' Nat concluded. 'Just wise, really.'

During the three years of their association, however, variety inexorably declined and it became a standing joke between the two men that posters outside theatres advertising *The Max Miller Show* were often pasted across with a strip announcing 'Closing – Last Week!' Once revered bastions of family entertainment were closing down, destined to become bingo halls, supermarkets, petrol stations, radio and television studios, or simply a pile of rubble. Moss Empire theatres, including

Shepherds Bush, Wood Green, Finsbury Park, New Cross and Woolwich, as well as Golders Green Hippodrome, were all to fall silent.

Nat Gonella also found it hard to break into television, which would have been an alternative employment in the 1950s, but in 1955 he did appear as a guest on the top-rated *Max Wall Show*. He and his host played a duet, 'I'll See You in My Dreams', with Wall on trombone.

The shows that Nat did with Miller and the television appearance with Max Wall were definite morale boosters for him but one with bandleader Ted Heath was a disaster. Heath's legendary orchestra was the foremost name in the British big band scene in the 1950s, and during its forty-five-year history created a legend with hit recordings (such as 'Hot Toddy', 'Blacksmith Blues', and 'Swingin' Shepherd Blues'), London Palladium concerts and premier radio and touring success. During the 1950s, Heath – a more than capable businessman – was fronting a consortium to buy up shares in the declining Selmer music empire. Gonella had formerly enjoyed a strong business association with Selmer, through advertising their trumpets, and had bought two thousand shares in the company. He finally agreed to sell them to Heath for double the price he had paid for them, plus a solo appearance on one of Heath's prestigious Sunday Palladium concerts. Such an appearance, thought the trumpeter, would do much to restore him to the music spotlight.

Before the concert, the Palladium was packed with crowds waiting to enjoy Heath's band-show and his trio of premier vocalists, Denis Lotis, Lita Roza and Dickie Valentine, a front-page heart-throb of the period. Gonella waited in the wings while Valentine did his solo spot including impressions of top singers, concluding with the newest rage 'cry-guy', Johnnie

Ray. Then – instead of introducing the trumpeter – Valentine announced the presence of Johnnie Ray himself in the theatre. A spotlight swept to a box above the stage occupied by the new American star and pandemonium erupted in which Valentine's subsequent introduction of Nat was all but lost amid the screams. Gonella strode on-stage to the introduction of 'Georgia on My Mind' and played as hard as he could while Ray continued to wave and blow kisses to fans from his box. At the last climactic note, not one ripple of applause greeted the performance and, after tackling a second tune and abandoning it midway, there was nothing for the despairing Gonella to do but walk disregarded from the stage on which, years before, he had received ecstatic receptions. History served to turn the tables, however. Johnnie Ray toured Britain again in 1984, long after the Beatles had changed the face of popular music for ever. Ticket sales were sparse and at one major venue, the Portsmouth Guildhall, not enough people applied to fill the first two rows of the theatre.

Things were bad for Nat Gonella. Where in the 1930s he had regularly earned a phenomenal seven hundred pounds a week, he was now glad of a few pounds simply to pay bills. Playing in seedy clubs and pubs, he shared dressing rooms with strippers and blue comedians, and sometimes travelled miles to remote country pubs to play in spaces no bigger than a living room. Working men's clubs were similarly soul-destroying and in one such venue in the north he was paid off, after his first set, by a cloth capped official with ten pounds and the comment that, 'We have better buglers in the town band.'

By the late 1950s Nat and Dorothy were living at Bitterne, an outer suburb of Southampton, where the trumpeter still scratched a living via club work. On one occasion he was asked to promote ticket sales for a concert by Duke Ellington, and in return was promised a meeting with the great bandleader. After the concert Nat was ushered into Ellington's dressing room. His host was affable enough, but disconcertingly remained completely naked throughout the conversation. Down to earth as ever, Nat told Ron Brown, 'Honest Ron, the Duke was starkers and kept saying how hot he was – I didn't know where to look!'

By this time, traditional jazz was booming and British bandleaders Kenny Ball, Acker Bilk and Chris Barber were invading the charts. But nobody, it seemed, even remembered Gonella now. The situation became very desperate and when a friend of Nat and Dorothy offered the trumpeter a part-time job in a bookmaker's office, he took it.

10

*The Music Goes Round and Round**

Despite his present cast-down state, Nat Gonella was determined to keep performing. Times had changed. Knocking at the door of popular music was a threatening new arrival, rock and roll. And twenty years had passed since he himself had been the equivalent of a latter-day rock idol. It was difficult to see which way to turn.

One night in March 1959, Nat's comeback began. On the table of his dressing room in a small theatre at Herne Bay, Kent, lay a good-luck telegram and a photograph from Louis Armstrong. Across the bottom of the photograph he had scrawled a timely message: 'To Nat, who I still think after all these years is a great musician and one of the greatest human beings that I have met in my whole life. God bless you Nat, and carry on with that horn. We have to stay around to keep these youngsters happy. Keep playing that music from the heart.'

Playing from the heart was something Gonella did naturally,

*Parlophone, Nat Gonella and his Georgians, 21.1.36

though exactly how to keep youngsters happy was more of a problem. Top hits of the time featured rock and rollers like Lloyd Price, Paul Anka, Eddie Cochran and the Coasters. There seemed little if any room for a man of fifty whose bill-topping era was thirty years in the past. The natural grit in Gonella, however, asserted itself. And that night, on a tiny stage in Herne Bay, he blew with all the fire and commitment that he could muster.

In summer 1959 the trumpeter took a five-piece band to Jersey, preceding the short overnight voyage with a one-nighter in Southampton. Their Jersey season was at the Rainbow Room, where they played for dancing and backed visiting cabaret acts, from pop singers to a troupe of Russian acrobats. Nat's long experience of variety made the job easier for him than for the rest of the band, but they busked their way through problems and no-one complained.

In Jersey Nat faced a serious and unfamiliar threat: lip trouble. According to some accounts his lip was completely paralysed but this is an understandable simplification; no trumpeter could play at all in such circumstances. Fatigue, the pressure of carrying a less competent group, or even mental depression may have caused the problem (which many trumpeters from Kenny Ball to Kenny Baker to Digby Fairweather have experienced in the course of their careers), but Gonella was able to continue playing. He confined himself to the trumpet's middle register and completed the season successfully. As time went by he found that jazz tunes were being requested more often and so built standards like 'St. Louis Blues' or 'Basin Street Blues' into his quintet's cabaret spot, to the audible pleasure of holiday-makers. Once again, jazz seemed to be attracting attention and when he returned to Southampton

Nat Gonella formed a jazz outfit to play around the south coast.

He had been thinking about the idea for two years at least. Longtime jazz promoter Ken Lindsay (who ran clubs at Hatfield, Barnet and elsewhere) had met Nat in the middle 1950s at Wood Green Empire to discuss a possible recording session, but nothing had come of the idea. Two years later, having heard that Gonella was thinking more seriously about returning to the jazz scene, Lindsay had re-approached him. This time Nat had agreed, and with record shop owner Doug Dobell, Lindsay had organised an *al fresco* jazz recording session at the Cottage Club, a famous musicians' haunt in London's Soho. Joining Gonella were members of Alex Welsh's band: Roy Crimmins (trombone), Archie Semple (clarinet), Fred Hunt (piano), Bill Reid (bass), John Richardson (drums), and the young Colin Smith who played trumpet behind Gonella on one track, 'Ain't Misbehavin''.

No doubt this session helped to refocus Gonella's attention on jazz, pure and simple. And, despite the vagaries of fashion, very few true jazz fans had forgotten his central contributions of twenty years before. In fact, to some degree, he had become a mysterious and intriguing figure whose disappearance into variety halls was felt as something of a loss. While he was away, a new, self-obsessed post-war generation had grown up. Arguments over the relative virtues of traditional and modern jazz raged, new stars emerged, and viewpoints were modified. But whenever Gonella did appear, the force of his talent, know-how and creative gifts made him seem like a teacher casting a cautionary glance at misbehaving pupils.

That was the effect of a 1959 album, *Salute to Satchmo*, by Nat Gonella's Strong-Arm Men, produced by Denis Preston for Columbia. On the record Gonella was teamed with a group of younger jazz stars in a quintet and his front-line partner was Tony Coe, arguably the greatest new swing saxophonist to emerge in Britain since Bruce Turner. Coe was then a youthful star of Humphrey Lyttelton's band. With a rhythm section composed of Lennie Felix (piano), Jack Fallon (bass) and Lennie Hastings (drums), the result was a hugely expert session in which no generation gap of any kind was audible. Bob Dawbarn's sleevenote looked forward to Gonella's re-emergence in jazz:

> Since the war Nat has had less than his share of the limelight. In the exciting days of the so-called New Orleans Revival in the 1940s – really the first showing of jazz as a popular music in Britain – the old established stars tended to be pushed into the background. [But] I for one hope that the success of this LP will encourage him to return to the scene with a band that does him full justice. In the short history of British jazz Nat Gonella may be a veteran but his playing still has the freshness and enthusiasm to match the men half his age.

Critics agreed. In the *Evening News*, Charles Fox, one of Britain's most highly respected jazz commentators, noted: 'British jazz has certainly leapt ahead since the days when Nat Gonella was leading his Georgians, but that does not make Nat a has-been! This LP shows that he has lost neither his lip nor his enthusiasm, and his tone seems to be warmer and more sensitive than it used to be. Dazzling Nat! More please!' Gerald Lascelles wrote in the *Tatler*: 'This happy-go-lucky record contains some of the most listenable jazz that I have heard from a recording studio in England!'

Bassist Jack Fallon had known Gonella from long before. As he told Digby Fairweather in 2004:

> I was in the Streamliners between August 1944 and July 1946 and we toured and broadcast, either from the Paris Cinema in Lower

Regent Street or Aeolian Hall – and he came in as a guest. He was very dapper and athletic and he played great. Then later we did the album with the Strong-Arm Men for Denis Preston. In the studio, I remember, he was proactive, aggressive. He talked and he played and he sang – he wasn't introvert at all. Like Wild Bill Davison, he attacked like a bull. I don't remember any aggravation or boredom at all. And I found him a very nice guy.

The time was as right as it ever could be for a Gonella return. Traditional jazz, as Dawbarn had noted, was experiencing its only true boom. More than ten years of groundwork laid by post-war revivalists, including George Webb, Humphrey Lyttelton, Freddy Randall and Chris Barber, had created a friendly ambiance for the music. And the emergence of younger stars such as Kenny Ball and Acker Bilk into the hit parade provided new icons for young people. Very soon, jazz would no longer be simply an underground music. It was about to become a fully-fledged popular music form with its own generation of fans who sent their heroes' records up the charts, packed their concerts and bought their fanzines. In short, traditional jazz was on the way to being big business.

Not all British musicians were happy to conform to the tenets of the 'trad boom'. Post-war leaders such as Humphrey Lyttelton, Sandy Brown and Al Fairweather, or Alex Welsh (all of whom had acquired fine reputations earlier in the 1950s) stood aside both from the stars and from the movement's excesses: strident banjoes, novelty material and too many vocals. Nevertheless, almost any competent traditional jazz band was a potential money-spinner. One of the most successful London agencies was run by Lyn Dutton, whose artists included Bilk and Ball as well as Alex Welsh and Humphrey Lyttelton. Dutton approached Gonella with a view to forming a new jazz band and, at only fifty-two-years-old, the trumpeter was ready to accept the offer.

The new group was to be called Nat Gonella and his Georgia Jazz Band and featured a classy team of post-war jazz stars: Teddy Layton (clarinet), Bobby Mickleburgh (trombone), Lennie Felix (piano), Alan Duddington (bass) and Lennie Hastings (drums). Modelled on Louis Armstrong's All Stars, the band made its debut on 6 February 1960 at Liverpool's legendary jazz club, the Cavern – later the home of the Beatles. Over five hundred teenagers attended the show, applauding wildly, and at its end Nat's reaction was brief but heartfelt: 'Oh man!' he said. 'It's great to be back!' The press agreed.

The band's repertoire included jazz standards such as 'Maryland, My Maryland', 'Didn't He Ramble', 'St. Louis Blues', 'Running Wild', 'Strutting with Some Barbecue', 'Slow Boat to China' and 'That's a Plenty', and packed a considerable punch. At first, however (possibly as a result of his sophisticated sidemen's views), Gonella refused to use a banjo in his line-up. This was no insignificant musical detail. 'Trad' depended on the banjo sound and it was a money-earner. One prominent London promoter, Roger Horton (longtime manager of the 100 Club at 100 Oxford Street), became famous for his adage: 'Show me a banjo and I'll show you a profit!' Later, Nat brought in a banjo, finding – as Bobby Hackett and plenty of other Americans found – nothing to dislike in the way the instrument can (in the right hands) swing a rhythm section. A more important problem, however unavoidable, was the lack of a hit record, the necessity for true stardom. As a consequence, Gonella occasionally found himself receiving requests for the hits of other, much younger, bandleaders. What, he must have wondered ruefully, about 'Nagasaki' or 'Oh! Mo'nah'? But most of the new jazz fans who packed the clubs had never heard of these old successes. In Louis Armstrong's words, it was time to take account of 'them generations'. 'They grow up so fast,' Armstrong would say, and Gonella in turn accepted the passage of time philosophically. Asked to play 'Summer Set', an Acker Bilk hit, he would good-humouredly respond that Acker had asked him not to play it for a week or two.

Gonella did in fact support Bilk's colossally successful Paramount Jazz Band on several occasions, including one prestigious concert at London's Royal Festival Hall, packed out with Bilk's fans. Gonella's versions of 'Mack the Knife' and 'Show Me the Way to Go Home' achieved an ovation which prompted one critic to head his review, fairly or not, as 'Too much Acker – not enough Nat!' Gonella also toured Sweden and Germany alongside Bilk's band and one night they visited a Hamburg beer garden. A German band was playing and when the bandmaster heard that Nat was in the crowd he invited him to conduct the band, then took him back to his table where two glasses of beer awaited them. Both men finished their drinks, after which Gonella was marched back to the podium; then back for more beer. The routine was repeated several times until Nat's baton was waving erratically and members of the band, who had similarly drunk deeply, were sounding off-colour. When Nat was finally allowed to sit down a buxom waitress presented him with a formidable bill. This apparently had been some kind of drinking contest, and the last person to finish his glass of beer paid for the round.

Nat's Georgia Jazz Band recorded only once, in 1960, a 45 r.p.m. single coupling 'My Gal Sal' and 'Show Me the Way to Go Home'. The playing is predictably excellent, but the band sound lacks the firm identity of a Kenny Ball or Acker Bilk and the record was not a commercial success. Thereafter, Gonella's management probably saw no urgent need to push him forward when newer jazz hit-makers abounded.

On 22 February 1960 Nat had an appointment at a London theatre to discuss a possible television show. On arriving, he recognised a few friends from the past and soon afterwards a large, very familiar Irishman, brandishing a big red book appeared. 'Nat Gonella,' said Eamonn Andrews, 'jazz pioneer and hero of a real-life stage romance, this is your life!' As the theatre doors opened and an audience swarmed in, Gonella, dumbfounded, was led away to get ready for the show. Listening carefully to the soundtrack reveals a *sotto voce* utterance: 'You sods!'

Guests on the *This Is Your Life* show included wife Dorothy (who told how she had courted Nat with new-laid eggs); George Latimer, his boyhood friend from St Mary's Guardian School; Fred Wood, from Archie Pitt's Busby Boys; Pat Smuts, Eddie Carroll and Lew Stone; plus recorded messages from Billy Kyle and Louis Armstrong. Helen Mack flew from California for the show. Humphrey Lyttelton also appeared, and when Andrews asked: 'What do you think of the new Nat Gonella?' Lyttelton retorted: 'Is this the new Nat Gonella? He hasn't even had a re-spray!' As the programme closed, Andrews invited Gonella to join Lyttelton and the Georgia Jazz Band for a flag-waving closer.

One sequel to the show was not so happy. Nat and his band were booked by Andrews to provide the music for the annual ball of the Irish Society in London. Gonella was dubious, as most of the music required might be unfamiliar, but pianist Lennie Felix assured him that all would be well. 'Just follow me,' he said, 'and busk.' The alcoholic evening passed smoothly enough until, at its climax, Andrews came to the microphone and requested that everyone should stand for the Irish

National Anthem. Neither Felix nor any other band member knew it and the evening thus reached an uncomfortable conclusion. Andrews was furious; on the telephone early next day he demanded an apology and refused to pay the band's fee for good measure.

In 1961 the Georgia Jazz Band was booked to appear on the popular religious television show, *Sunday Break*, which combined theological discussion with popular music of the time. Ron Brown saw the show and observed that at one minute on the screen there was a serious discussion about religion and the next there were Nat and the boys blowing hot jazz. The contrast amused the trumpeter; in his early career, virtuous ministers were still able to preach that jazz was 'the music of the Devil'.

Television and radio bookings served to confirm that Gonella was back and newspapers and magazines were eager to interview him. *Jazz Journal*, then edited by Sinclair Traill, particularly welcomed his return. In January 1960, critic Graham Boatfield reviewed his *Salute to Satchmo* collection in favourable terms and in March the magazine ran a full feature by Brian Gladwell (illustrated with a first-class photographic action shot by Beryl Bryden) titled 'The Return of Nat Gonella'. Gladwell summed up the general feelings of the jazz community with a simple final paragraph: 'To welcome Nat Gonella back on the British jazz scene is a long overdue pleasure. He should never have been away.' Two years later the magazine featured Gonella again, this time in their 'In My Opinion' column, a feature devoted to reviews of current records by musicians.

The popular press also sought out Gonella for his views on various burning issues including rock and roll: 'Well, people are making a lot of money out of it so it can't be all bad.'

Modern jazz: 'Most of it is too sad and serious. It can be clever in its way but jazz to me means happiness.' Money: 'Now there's a subject! Possibly, if I'd had a better education, I would have been more sensible with it. But I had to learn about money the hard way.' And snobs: 'I always put on my best Cockney accent; this usually embarrasses them and they soon go away.'

The early 1960s were certainly a visible (and audible) period of renaissance for Gonella and his sidemen. Teddy Layton was a fine clarinettist who worked with great revivalists, including Mike Daniels and Eric Silk, before forming his own band in 1956 to debut at a concert in aid of the Hungarian Relief Fund at Battersea Town Hall. Later he worked principally on the south coast and assembled the band for Nat Gonella's funeral ceremony. Alan Duddington (still playing regularly in the West Country) had been a sideman with Mick Mulligan's band, and Lennie Felix, a one-time British jazz celebrity who died in 1980, was a respected pianist with solo albums to his credit. Bobby Mickleburgh (like Duddington, still active) was a hugely gifted multi-instrumentalist who doubled on trumpet, trombone and sousaphone; his career had included seasons with Eddie Carroll and Lou Preager in the 1940s and later work with first-class bands including Freddy Randall, Sid Phillips and Bruce Turner.

Drummer Lennie Hastings joined Gonella between two long stints with Alex Welsh's band. A graduate of the bebop years who turned to dixieland music early on for preference (with Freddy Randall's band), he had immense respect for Gonella. 'I'd taken my own band to Germany,' he told Digby Fairweather in 1976:

> and it was a good band but I was let down by an agent who had promised me work if I came back to Britain. So I was stuck back

> in Britain without anything lined up. Then Lyn Dutton's agency asked me if I was interested in making a come-back with Nat Gonella. I accepted immediately. It was great; he was marvellous to work with, very easy-going and a gentleman. I'll never forget one night at the 100 Club. All the young trumpet turks were on-stage blowing their brains out: guys like Mike Cotton, Kenny Ball and Colin Smith. Then Nat came on with his horn and absolutely showed them all the way home – playing marvellously.

Alan Duddington also emphasised the superior nature of Gonella's performance to Digby Fairweather. 'He had this completely outstanding sound. All I can describe it as is an *American* sound. Full, fat and broad.'

In February 1961 Nat recorded again for Denis Preston. This time the album – based on Louis Armstrong's luxurious four volume *Autobiography* boxed set of four years earlier and complete with the spoken links that Armstrong had introduced – was called *The Nat Gonella Story*. With three different groups (including a nine-piece band arranged by Kenny Graham), the trumpeter re-created fourteen of his most famous hits in a contemporary setting which included Stan Tracey on both piano and vibraphone and first-call trombonist Don Lusher, as well as Tony Coe, Jimmy Skidmore and Joe Temperley (the saxophone section of Humphrey Lyttelton's band), plus a variety of respected contemporary jazz and session men. Gonella's own sleevenote confirmed his enthusiasm for the result. 'I've never played better – nor in better company,' he said, taking space to praise Coe's featured contributions and Graham's sparkling arrangements. The LP (reissued in 1977) was unquestionably an artistic success. Subsequently, a copy was sent to Armstrong himself who acknowledged it with a letter. '*The Nat Gonella Story* was just great – sounded wonderful,' said the master. 'Also your band. You are blowing good and solid as ever.

More power to "ye" Daddy. Your boy – Satch.' Gonella was proud of the letter and had it framed alongside Armstrong's famous diet sheet 'Lose weight – the Satchmo way!' The recording was unquestionably an artistic success, but what it was not was 'trad'. It sounds far more like the contemporary mainstream output of Humphrey Lyttelton's band and as such stood no chance of wide sales; a less artistic concept than Preston's might have cashed in on the booming market of the time. But even such a commercial ploy might have failed and in any case the Beatles were on their way up. Perhaps British jazz history benefited from the fact that things went the way they did.

During the early 1960s Gonella travelled widely again to play one-nighters with his Georgia Jazz Band and – from 1961–62 – as guest star with clarinettist Doug Richford's London Jazzmen. Despite his association with the 'trad boom', Richford was already forty-years-old by the time it broke and had played with many bands previously including that of Gonella himself. In 1959 he joined boom-star Bob Wallis until 1961, then formed his own band. Trumpeter John Hodgkins (who preceded Gonella in Richford's group) points out that the clarinettist would have grown up listening to Gonella's Georgians in the 1930s and would have been well aware of the trumpeter's commercial potential, hence his billing of Nat as 'special guest'. With Richford, Gonella played jazz clubs and RAF camps, singing old hits like 'The Isle of Capri'. He also recorded a single in January 1962: 'Yip-I-Addy-I-Ay' backed with 'On Sunday I Go Sailing'.

At the beginning of the 1960s, motorways were not yet built in Britain and travelling was even more tiring than it is today, especially for a man of over fifty. Dorothy Gonella worried about her husband but recognised that earning money was still essential. As Nat put it, 'There's no company pension in show business.' Following a Saturday gig in Nottingham, Nat did not arrive home until five o'clock in the morning; his first words to a half-asleep Dorothy were, 'What a catastrophe.' He undressed still muttering, 'What a catastrophe,' and by this time she was wide awake. 'What catastrophe?' she asked anxiously. The late arrival shook his head. 'What Blackburn did to Spurs yesterday.'

Nat still managed to find time for golf and as a member of the Vaudeville Golfing Society (a show-business club with strictly limited membership) he played regular rounds with fellow entertainers. In a tournament at Leeds his opponent was Harry Secombe and, as they were about to tee off, Secombe inexplicably presented his opponent with a dozen new golf balls. 'Well,' Gonella told Ron Brown, 'after such a generous gesture I couldn't beat him, could I?' Another time he enjoyed a game with Max Bygraves and, after it was over, Bygraves suggested they should have a meal. Together the two men headed for an up-market restaurant but hardly had they made their entrance when the head waiter informed Bygraves that as he was not wearing a tie he would not be able to dine; Mr Gonella, however, who was suitably dressed, might remain.

When Nat became a victim of angina in later years he rescinded his membership of the Vaudeville Golfing Society to let a new member join. But once a year the society held a members' stag night, giving performers the chance to let their hair down – sometimes with blue material. At one such night, at the Park Lane Hotel in 1961, Nat was asked to provide a musical spot and corralled fellow trumpeters Eddie Calvert and Roy Castle, together with the three King Brothers, to join him on-stage for a fifteen-minute session. They finished with a parody of the Temperance Seven, then riding high with their hit record 'You're Driving Me Crazy' and afterwards one thousand people gave them a standing ovation.

As the 1960s progressed, rock and roll – which most jazz musicians and (serious) critics had dismissed as light and fluffy fare – was about to bring in its heaviest artillery, the Beatles, and popular culture would soon be purged of most of its old influences. Clarinettist Henry Mackenzie, a long-time cornerman of Ted Heath's orchestra, told Digby Fairweather, 'When we went north we were used to crowds gathering round the stand as Ted played. And sometimes there would be a little group at the other end of the hall. As the 1960s gathered speed we got used to crowds gathering at the other end of the hall instead… paying no attention to us.' Giants of popular music such as Heath were dismayed, seeing every principle for which they stood – technical skill, creative flare and meticulous high standards – apparently swept away by importunate juniors whose music was irresistible to a new generation.

The newcomers included John Lennon, who said openly, 'We hated the jazz bands at the Cavern.' Nat Gonella – as a survivor from a previous jazz generation anyhow – now had two strikes against him. Former stars of the trad boom found themselves relegated to cabaret and jazz clubs and barred from the hit parade; one unfortunate, trumpeter Bob Wallis, emerged from a year-long residency at the London Palladium after hit records to find himself virtually unemployable. Nat Gonella faced comparable problems. The Georgia Jazz Band disbanded and he returned to playing in clubs and pubs, grateful for a booking in any surviving variety hall. By this time, pit orchestras, where they still existed, had dwindled in size and the quality of players diminished in parallel. 'Man,' said Nat, 'you just can't imagine what emerges from an orchestra pit. I couldn't stand the awful row and I had to blow like hell to try and drown it!'

Yet, even in these conditions, Nat saw new jazz talent continuing to emerge. In 1965 he first championed the young trumpeter Bruce Adams – now one of Britain's most exceptional players. 'My father had been a friend of Nat's from the 1930s,' Adams told Fairweather in 2004:

> He was known as Bobby Bruce, one of a singing duo with Jack Payne's band in 1936, and he and Nat used to bump into each other regularly on the halls. I first met Nat in 1963 when he was on the bill at the King's Theatre, Glasgow, with Ellis Jackson who at the time was eighty-three but only owned up to being seventy-five, and used to end his act double-somersaulting across the stage. Anyhow, Nat sponsored me on *Opportunity Knocks!* in 1965 and I won the first one, then went back and did three more before Nat came on with me for the last one, where we played 'Georgia on My Mind' together. I was fourteen at the time! Nat was lovely, very sweet, very kind – and very encouraging to young players too.
>
> I remember that he was also in variety at the Glasgow Pavilion – which is still there – with the comedian Johnny Victory. In one of the sketches Nat had to dress up as a wounded soldier and came on with all the tomato sauce to play the last post in a kilt! And, of course, he'd kick up his leg, and the audience just loved him. He was a great showman. When that show was on, bookies still hadn't been legalised and Nat was betting every day, and one night the Pavilion was raided. And the management had to beg the police to let him out of the wagon – which they did, of course!
>
> A bit later on we used to go together to sit in with Sam Greenall's Ribble Valley Jazzmen in Preston. But around that time he started to get a few problems. At one point he had a slight seizure and the doctor said, 'No more blowing for the time being – and no more backing the horses, too, because of the tension.' And by the time I got to know him he had a few lip problems, just

slight difficulties getting certain things to work. It might have had to do with that old Pardubah mouthpiece he used; cushion rims sometimes can trap your lip – there's no room to move – and he might have damaged his lip a little, I think. But, of course, Harry James had given him the Pardubah, you see. We stayed in touch until he moved down south to Gosport, but he wasn't a great letter-writer; I think Dorothy used to do most of that. And, of course, the last time I saw – and played with – him was with your band not long before he died.

In 1965 Gonella visited a studio to take part in a recording of selections from Lionel Bart's score of *Oliver!* with the Mayfair Theatre Orchestra and children from the Corona Stage School. Gonella's co-stars included Michael Wennick, Leslie Fyson, David Rosen, Rita Cameron and Peter Brittle, and for this budget-label undertaking (on the Presto label marketed through Woolworth's stores, and now understandably rare) he sang a convincing version of 'Reviewing the Situation'. Then, on 1 August 1966, he was back at the BBC to guest on Roy Plomley's *Desert Island Discs*. His choices brought few surprises: three from Louis Armstrong ('Basin Street Blues', 'Wild Man Blues' and 'Georgia on My Mind') plus 'Trumpet Blues and Cantabile' by Harry James, 'I'm Comin' Virginia' with Bix Beiderbecke, and (perhaps surprisingly) Roy Fox's 'Whispering'. His two remaining choices were classical items: Handel's 'Hallelujah Chorus' sung by the Huddersfield Choral Society with the Royal Liverpool Philharmonic, and Dame Maria Callas singing Verdi's 'O don fatale'. For a book he chose *The Collected Stories of Damon Runyon* and for his luxury a set of golf clubs and balls.

Most of Nat's work opportunities were now in the north of England and this prompted him to move with Dorothy to a small modern bungalow in Matterdale Road, Leyland,

Lancashire. A few miles south of Preston, it served as a base from which he could reach local jazz clubs, working-men's clubs and summer season shows in nearby Blackpool. Now in his sixties, he was considered to have reached veteran status and accordingly was invited to join the cast of Liverpool impresario Don Ellis' *Those Were the Days* revue, which toured nationally. Others on the bill included impressionist Peter Cavanagh, Welsh comedienne Gladys Morgan and Adelaide Hall, the legendary performer whose career in jazz and show business was as long as Nat's own. A second such review in which Gonella both played and sang was at the Wimbledon Theatre. It was the BBC's *Old Time Music Hall* presentation and starred the trumpeter with the veteran music-hall and radio stars Elsie and Doris Waters.

During his Blackpool visits in the late 1960s and early 1970s Nat also renewed acquaintance with wrestler Jack Pye who, with his brothers, instilled fear into opponents nationally in both pre- and post-war years. Always a great lover of wrestling, Nat played regularly at Pye's nightclub in the city and also often sat in with Sam Greenall's band in Preston. He was becoming more loath to travel, however, and regularly turned down offers to return to London or to record. One such offer came from Digby Fairweather, who had liaised with band-leader Steve Lane to record an album with Gonella for Lane's Halcyon label. Another came from promoter Michael Webber who, in 1970, presented the first of a series of concert salutes to Louis Armstrong – this one to honour Armstrong's seventi-eth birthday – featuring Alex Welsh, Humphrey Lyttelton, George Chisholm, Beryl Bryden, John Chilton and a host of guest stars. Nat was asked to introduce the concert. John Wortham recalls: 'I lived at Maidenhead at the time and had already written to Nat and talked to him on the phone for a year or two; he was always very chatty. Then I read in the *Melody Maker*, that he was coming to London to introduce this great concert and gave Michael Webber a ring. As Maidenhead was only twenty-five miles west of London and Nat was still in Leyland, I suggested that Nat might stay with my wife Anna and myself. Then unexpectedly he collapsed on stage somewhere up north – which also made the *Melody Maker*, I think – and couldn't appear.'

Then, out of the blue, came a call from Holland. It was from Ted Easton, his contact of twenty years before. After the Americans had disbanded their bases, Easton had developed his technique as a drummer and formed a jazz band as well as opening a state-of-the-art jazz club in Scheveningen, the scene of Nat's visit with Ray Noble forty years previously. The silver-haired Easton was now a celebrity (as well as a seasoned businessman) and ran a thriving record company, Riff, which was in the midst of amassing a formidable catalogue of new recordings by vintage American jazz stars who were regular guests at his club. The purpose of his call was to ask if Nat would appear at his club as guest performer. At first the trumpeter was doubtful but Dorothy persuaded him to accept the invitation and laid out his dress suit accordingly.

On arrival, Nat met Easton and immediately set about rehearsing an act. Easton enterprisingly suggested 'Oh! Mo'nah', a tune Gonella had rarely aired in years. The idea turned out to be a stroke of inspiration. Dutch fans loved the song, with its cheery sing-along chorus, and called for several encores every night. Word quickly spread that Nat Gonella was back in town and drawing capacity crowds, and subsequently a team of recording engineers appeared to record his music for Easton, with the intention of including 'Oh! Mo'nah' on an album. Ted paid Nat and so far as the trumpeter was concerned that would be the end of the matter. Soon afterwards he went home.

On 7 March 1973 Nat Gonella reached the age of sixty-five, announced his retirement from the entertainment profession and reported to the Leyland Post Office to collect his pension. At this point it seemed possible that his name was destined to fade into show-business history. But then Easton rang again. Could Nat come back to Holland right away? His record company had released 'Oh! Mo'nah' as a single and it had reached number five in the Dutch hit parade. In the post-rock days of the 1970s this was nothing short of miraculous; out came the dress suit and once again Nat flew to Holland. When his plane touched down the trumpeter received a welcome fit for a Hollywood superstar and he was driven directly to Scheveningen to meet the city's mayor, who officially crowned him 'King of Jazz'. While two pretty girls kissed him and presented him with the first of several bouquets, an impressive medal decorated with red, white and blue ribbon was hung around his neck. It was a triumphant return for the new superstar, who typically enough was heard to enquire if the medal was accompanied by twenty thousand gilders a year!

During his second stay Nat played with musicians from Easton's stable of American guests, including tenorists Bud Freeman and Buddy Tate, cornettist Wild Bill Davison, altohornist/pianist/trumpeter Dick Cary, and clarinettists Peanuts Hucko and Bob Wilber, Gonella's own preferred partner. Before one concert across the border in Belgium (to which the musicians travelled in Easton's car), they found that all local cafes and restaurants had closed for the night and it was suggested that a station sandwich machine might do. But, having located a machine, none of the party had Belgian coins with which to feed it. Nat delved into his pocket and found a Dutch coin, which he handed to Bud Freeman. 'Try this,' he suggested. To their amazement, the machine emptied its contents in all directions, and when it eventually stopped there were sandwiches for all.

During his Dutch visits Nat was sometimes the guest of an electronics-cum-mechanical wizard, Frits van t'Hof, banjoist with Easton's band. On one occasion in the early morning, Nat crept down a spiral staircase as quietly as possible to visit a lavatory. On opening the door, he was greeted by a double-forte recording of 'Brahms' Lullaby', one of Frits' mechanical surprises. The following morning, in the garden he was offered a cup of coffee by his host, who then produced a control panel and flicked switches. A small model train left the garage, traversed tracks around the garden and then glided to a halt by the two men, carrying two cups of coffee and a box of biscuits on a truck.

During one concert Nat shared billing with singer Beryl Bryden. Once again, fortunately, a recording unit was on hand to record rousing selections including 'Bill Bailey Won't You Please Come Home?' and 'A Hot Time in the Old Town Tonight' amid twelve tracks. Easton's recorded output at the time was prolific and on his trips to Holland Gonella recorded four more LPs for him: invaluable documentation of his later playing. These comprised: *When You're Smiling* (recorded live with Bryden at Easton's New Orleans Club in January 1970) and three more from 1975: *My Favourite Things* (on 7 May, produced by Peter Schilperoort, leader of the renowned Dutch Swing College Band, who also played piano on one track, 'Lazybones'); *The Music Goes Round and Round* (31 May) and *Wishing You a Swinging Christmas* (October) for which, along with Easton's band, he was joined by Dick Cary on piano.

Nat remembered one moment in Scheveningen for the rest

of his life. One morning he was drinking coffee outside a cafe when a nearby radio played his hit record of 'Oh! Mo'nah'. A group of children playing in the square stopped to dance and sing along to the music; the sight moved the trumpeter until he was close to tears.

In 1975, at the end of his five-year collaboration with Easton, Gonella flew home to Lancashire. Now it really seemed as if the quiet life would take over; his days were filled with gardening, dog-walking, a daily visit to the betting shop, playing records and meeting friends. But still it seemed strange. Nat Gonella, so recently a star on the Continent, was living in semi-obscurity in his homeland.

11

*Farewell Blues**

Throughout his long life, and even at low points in his career, Gonella always took pride in his trumpet technique and level of performance. As a perfectionist, and his own severest critic, he knew that in the later days of his Holland visits he was no longer playing to his own satisfaction. A highly capable second trumpeter (Bob Wulffers) had been on hand in Easton's band, and latterly Gonella had been happy to lean more heavily on singing and Wulffers' musical support. Now in his sixties, he was finding it more difficult to play to his own high standards.

His decision finally to conclude a lifelong love affair with his instrument was literally a 'throwaway' decision, made while on a visit with Dorothy to daughter Natalie in Bristol. 'I decided to throw it off the Clifton suspension bridge,' he told Digby Fairweather. 'See it go down into the mud, spla-a-at! And that would be that.' (The scene recalls a cameo in *The Five Pennies*, a 1959 Paramount biopic of cornettist Red Nichols, starring

*Parlophone, Nat Gonella and his Georgians, 24.7.35

Danny Kaye, in which the cornettist throws his instrument from the San Francisco Bay Bridge.) Natalie (who had been 'Miss Bristol' in 1953) wanted no part of the plan, however, and determinedly rescued the trumpet. It would remain at her house until after her father's death when, auctioned at Bonham's, it reached the reserve price of three thousand pounds on sale to a close friend and Gonella collector from Gosport, John Pittard.

Although comfortable enough in Leyland, Nat and Dorothy now considered a move back to the south coast. The trumpeter had regularly worked there throughout his career and Dorothy had grown up in Gosport. Nestling on the western shores of Portsmouth harbour, the pleasant town serves as dormitory for the Royal Naval Base and Portsmouth Dockyard. Dorothy still had relatives living there. So the decision was made: the couple would leave Lancashire to spend their retirement in Hampshire. Accordingly, in 1977, they moved into a modest terrace cottage at 81 Clayhall Road, handy for the town's centre or the seafront of Stokes Bay, overlooking the Solent. Few local residents were aware that a celebrity was now in their midst, although the (now defunct) *Gosport Standard* ran a short feature on the new arrival.

At that time Digby Fairweather wrote a short piece for the house magazine of London's Pizza Express in his regular 'Digby's Column'. It pointed out how overlooked Gonella was in Britain, with very few reissues, and no book about him. To Fairweather's enormous surprise, one night while working at the club he was handed an envelope by Monty Montgomery, Gonella's one-time lead trumpeter and by then a respected Pizza Express *habitué*. In it was a handwritten letter from Nat, thanking him. The article and its note of thanks are preserved in two frames on Fairweather's wall.

Then, in 1978, the proprietors of the Park Hotel, Alverstoke, decided to experiment with live jazz nights. Ron Brown covered the first of them for the *Gosport Standard*. 'It was certainly a pleasant enough session of traditional jazz,' he wrote, 'by Doug and Dory Whitfield's Riverside Jazz Band. [But] as the evening progressed a buzz went round the room that Nat Gonella was on the premises.' A delighted Whitfield introduced the star, who readily agreed to sing 'When You're Smiling' followed by his signature tune 'Georgia on My Mind'. It completed an unforgettable evening. When Brown returned to the Park the following Thursday he was forced to stand all evening; the room was thronged with fans hoping to catch a glimpse of Gonella again. From then on the one-time trumpeter became a regular at the Park Hotel, turning up to sing with south coast jazz bands including the Riverside and Gateway, clarinettist Chris Walker's quintet and trumpeter Cuff Billett's Olympia Jazz Band. Hearing him often there, Ron Brown noted that, although he no longer played the trumpet, his voice was better than ever, probably because, not having to worry about playing the horn, he could develop his singing style and actually improve on the same songs that he had sung for so many years. A good example was his version of 'St. James Infirmary Blues', delivered with a comedy timing worthy of Max Miller.

Gradually, well-known names from the jazz world made the pilgrimage to Gosport with their own bands or as guest performers. Their prime reason was to meet or renew acquaintance with Gonella. He was delighted, and memorable sessions ensued with Monty Sunshine, Pete Allen and Fairweather, who recalls:

> I'd heard about the sessions from my old friend Chris Walker who let me in on what was really a semi-secret: that Nat was regularly

> at the Park. I was grateful and thrilled and one day my mother and I drove first to Portsmouth – where I picked up a brand-new Getzen cornet from Gabriel's Horn House, a local brass specialist – and then on to the Park. Nat arrived with friends but found time to talk at the bar. I couldn't believe how down-to-earth he was, devoid of so-called 'star syndrome'. Later I played with him too – which was fairly unnerving.

Those early events are fondly remembered by Gosport jazz fans, who quickly took Gonella to their hearts. Fairweather came down from London again, bringing with him friends and musical colleagues from Gonella's early days, including bassist Tiny Winters and tenorist Pat Smuts. Both men were still musically active, Smuts as a gigging musician, Winters as occasional leader of his Palm Court Trio at the National Theatre. Gonella and Winters had stayed in touch through occasional telephone calls and letters, but to see them together, as Ron Brown remembers, was magic; they sparked off each other's memories of their legendary tenure with Lew Stone at the Monseigneur. During one of Winters' Gosport visits he and Nat re-created a two-man version of Stone's legendary 'Little Nell' routine, and Fairweather presented Nat and Dorothy Gonella with trophies; one engraved with 'Nat Gonella, King of Jazz', the other with the Hoagy Carmichael title 'For Every Man There's a Woman'.

Boosted by Nat's presence, the Gosport Jazz Club, as it became known, moved from strength to strength. A growing army of jazz followers came to enjoy such 'strictly traditional' names as Ken Colyer, Alan Elsdon, Monty Sunshine, Steve Lane, Max Collie, Harry Gold, Kenny Ball, Pete Allen, Yank Lawson, Dick Charlesworth, Jim Shepherd, Mike Daniels, Rusty Taylor, Maxine Daniels, Digby Fairweather and Beryl Bryden; a formidable bill of musical fare. Such sessions, however, regularly sped into overdrive when Nat Gonella left his specially designated 'guest table' to join the bands to sing. He was at his best when performing duets with Bryden, Taylor or Daniels, who would never think of finishing their acts without him.

In 1982 Digby Fairweather, a Gonella fan from boyhood, embarked on a national tour with his band dedicated to Gonella's music and titled *We Remember Nat*. The band featured Fairweather (trumpet/cornet), Pete Strange (trombone), John Barnes (reeds), Paul Sealey (guitar/banjo), Jack Fallon (bass) and John Armatage (drums), plus guest Tiny Winters on bass. It played venues countrywide. But it was not until the show came to Gosport that the subject of the tribute was able to join them on-stage.

Later the show was recorded for the American label Jazzology. Fairweather recalls:

> I'd checked keys with Nat and we recorded backing tracks plus our instrumentals at Ted Taylor's Porcupine Studios in Mottingham [in Kent]. Afterwards I sent a cassette down to Nat just to show him the backings and was disappointed when Liza Lincoln, my partner of the time – and the singer in the show – told me that Nat had rung and said 'I can't do it.' Later on I realised what had happened. He thought he had to dub the vocals on to the cassette – or on to another one, using mine as a backing track – at home! Naturally he had to give up. But it wasn't till years later that I played Nat's tape back and heard him valiantly wrestling with the problem on a home recorder. At the end, when he'd given up, he sang a little bit of 'Ragtime Cowboy Joe' on to the cassette unaccompanied and when I heard it we said, 'Let's put it on the CD anyhow.' Wild Bill Davison had dubbed Nat's vocals meantime, but we thought, 'how great to have even a little of the sound of Nat's voice on the CD.' But the pressing people who cut the disc didn't do it. So the CD has 'A Few Words from

Nat' as its last track – and it's not there! It just wasn't meant to be.'

Ron Brown's articles and reviews in newspapers and magazines, plus the first edition of this biography, revealed more about Nat's life. His daughter Natalie told Fairweather in 2002: 'I was always proud of my father, but it wasn't until reading the first biography in 1985 that I fully realised what a roller-coaster life he'd led, and maybe why we'd seen so little of each other.'

Regular radio coverage (Alan Dell's *Dance Band Days*, Gerry Didymus' *78 Nostalgia Show* and Chris Walker's *Jazz on Solent*) ensured that Gonella's name was truly back in the limelight all over the south coast and beyond. The late jazz presenter Tim Colwell also featured Nat in a two-hour special tribute show, based on *This is Your Life*, on Portsmouth's commercial station, Radio Victory. It was also noticeable that the sparse Gonella discography of previous years was now regularly augmented by reissue LPs on EMI, Decca, Philips and Saville.

Then in 1984, Fairweather – noticing a television programme celebrating *Thirty Years of Humphrey Lyttelton* produced for Channel 4 – telephoned the producer, Laurence Vulliamy, to ask whether *Fifty Years of Nat Gonella* might not be an appropriate follow-up. Vulliamy agreed and the show was recorded on Southsea's South Parade Pier (where the Georgians had performed many times in the 1930s) on 1 April 1985; fifty years to the day after the formation of Gonella's first band. Compered by Benny Green, the programme featured the band Fairweather had led for his *We Remember Nat* tour, fronted by Nat in top form, singing an hour's worth of his hits. Humphrey Lyttelton, disguised in a tiger suit for his walk-on, joined Gonella and the band for a concluding tear-up on 'Tiger Rag'. Green also recorded interviews with Winters, Pat Smuts and Joyce Stone but these were not included in the eventual transmission. Nor was the song 'I Must See Annie Tonight', which Fairweather had rearranged from Gonella's original American recording of 1939. The tricky lyrics prompted several false starts, by which time the audience was rocking with good-natured laughter. Later on, at Gosport, the song's difficulty would become a standing joke between Gonella and his audience. 'What do you want me to sing next?' he would enquire, to receive the universal roared response: 'I Must See Annie Tonight'!

On recording day, South Parade Pier was besieged with television mobile wagons, technicians running back and forth with cameras and microphones, and cables everywhere. Someone asked a member of Fairweather's band, John Barnes, 'What's all the fuss?' Barnes explained that a TV special was being filmed, starring Nat Gonella.

'Oh,' said the inquirer, 'I thought they must be filming the *Antiques Road Show*.'

'You're not so far wrong,' chuckled the saxophonist.

Gonella was not keen on television appearances in his later years (in fact he had light-heartedly threatened Vulliamy that he might be too busy in the betting shop to record his show). This aversion could be traced to the day when a BBC unit had gone to his house in Leyland to film a programme about his life. The disruption to his home was considerable and put him off the idea. This was apparent when Ron Brown was approached by producer David Kenten of Anglia Television to try and persuade Gonella to grant a two-minute interview. Kenten's series was *Bygones* and previous subjects had included comedian Tommy Trinder and music hall trio Wilson, Keppel and Betty. Now he was compiling a programme about West End nightclub life of the 1930s and wanted Gonella to provide memories of the period. Brown asked Nat, whose first reply was an emphatic, 'No.' But Brown persisted. The interview would be just two minutes long, only cameraman, soundman and interviewer would be present and the whole thing would take place at Brown's house. Reluctantly, the trumpeter agreed.

The day arrived and Brown drove to collect Gonella. All was well until he returned with his guest to find a circus had been set up. The Anglia team had travelled from Norwich with cars, vans and crew, bearing an array of sound, lighting and film equipment and Gonella, shocked at the chaos, asked to be returned home immediately. Horrified at the thought of telling Kenten that his interview was cancelled, Brown turned on the persuasion: the crew was already on-site, the interview might as well proceed and, after all, only two minutes were involved. Eventually Gonella agreed and Brown bundled him out of the car and into the chaotic house, where an army of engineers was transforming his sitting room into a television studio.

Fortunately Kenten was quick to spot the developing problem. After introductions he sat his guest in an armchair; lighting and sound were finalised and Brown was unexpectedly instructed to interview his guest. No-one had mentioned this previously, but Brown, without script or time for thought, manufactured questions ad lib while the cameras rolled. Whenever he paused, Kenten urged, 'Keep going!' and the two-minute interview lasted for four hours. Gonella took it all in his stride, producing a fund of stories and anecdotes. By the time producer and crew were sure they had sufficient footage, Nat looked as fresh as when they had begun the exercise, while Brown was an exhausted wreck. But it was worth it, he'd thought. The Anglia outfit and David Kenten did a marvellous job producing a thirty minute documentary, which included rare footage of the Georgians.

Nat was less opposed to radio as long as he was not asked to leave Gosport and the now-ailing Dorothy. To mark his eightieth birthday, Richard Willcox, producer of the nineteen-year Radio 2 series *Jazz Score*, brought his show to Gosport Jazz Club to record two editions. A capacity audience packed the club to see and hear chairman Benny Green put questions to his two teams, the 'Veterans' (represented by Nat Gonella and respected veteran jazz critic Max Jones) and the 'Youngsters' represented by trumpeters Alan Elsdon and Digby Fairweather. For the record, the Veterans won the first show while the Youngsters triumphed in the second in two closely fought contests. As ever, the stories, not the points, were the show's true raison d'être. And one of the show's highlights occurred when the club phone rang unexpectedly. 'If it's a gig,' Elsdon ad libbed, 'I'll take it!'

One more unusual radio broadcast featuring Gonella was transmitted on 22 September 1987. A twenty-minute play for the BBC's Children's Education programme was titled *Just like Nat Gonella*, and the story concerned the efforts of a young boy to acquire an old trumpet he had seen in a junk shop window. The storyline was based on Nat's early errand-boy experience and the production was laced with extracts from original Gonella recordings.

Ron Brown was a regular visitor to the Gonella home and became aware of the loving partnership that Nat and Dorothy Gonella had developed over the years. Dorothy had an excellent memory and could relate stories of bandleaders and variety performers with whom Nat had shared billing.

During the day, when not on his regular expedition to the

bookmaker's, the now-ageing trumpeter could often be found sitting in the old wooden shed at the end of his garden, listening to tapes from his jazz and dance band collection, most of them gifts from fans or record producers. A fly on the wall, Ron Brown observed at the time, would have seen his lips moving along to the music, for what he was doing was either learning or brushing up on the words of various songs, accumulated over more than six decades as a performer. Nat would often surprise his Gosport audiences – as well as his accompanists – by producing a new song. It was more than possible that he had never sung it until the night in question, and such moments could usefully have been preserved on record. The surprise of the band supporting him was witnessed by Brown. They had to be alert, for Nat would sometimes commence with one song and develop it into a medley of three others. Good musicians took it in their stride while others were completely baffled.

A garden shed therefore became Nat Gonella's study and rehearsal room. As to actual gardening, however, his approach was basic. 'I put the seeds in, Ron,' he told Brown, 'and if they come up, great! If they don't – bugger 'em!'

The modest size of Gonella's house might perhaps have surprised fans who remembered the trumpeter's glory days as one of Britain's highest-paid entertainers, but he had always been a heavy gambler and seldom bothered to save. Now, though, money – or lack of it – never seemed to worry him. Nat Gonella retained his happy-go-lucky acceptance of whatever life handed or took away from him with no surrender to self-pity. This sometimes frustrated his wife Dorothy who – knowing that he had regularly been short-changed by bookers and agents, especially later on in his career – was protective of her husband and quick to recognise those who sought to take advantage of him. It could be argued, Brown felt, that Nat had, to some degree, been short-changed by fate: by the onset of war at the height of his career and the onset of the Beatles when he was firmly re-establishing his reputation in jazz. But bitterness was no part of his make-up. And when he had money, Nat, like Louis Armstrong, would often pass it on to someone less fortunate. When challenged by Dorothy he would say resignedly: 'Well, he's a fellow musician, down on his luck.' Sadly, when Nat had been down on his luck there was often no-one to offer such kindnesses in exchange. But in Gosport Nat and Dorothy found genuine friends.

Although by now reluctant to leave Dorothy for long, the trumpeter could occasionally be persuaded to travel out of Gosport for a jazz treat. For one such, his friend Bob Panting (a retired bank manager) hired a mini-bus to drive Nat and fans to a theatre near Newbury, Berkshire, to see the popular touring show *Jazzin' Around*. A vehicle for Pete Allen's Jazz Band, this revue featured guest stars including (at various times) Tommy Burton, Beryl Bryden and Edna Savage. Ron Brown was in the party and remembers that it was a great night and Nat was in fine form. But the journey home turned into something of a nightmare, for the mini-bus broke down in Twyford, just south of Winchester. It was a struggle pushing the vehicle to a safe place but thankfully there was a pub near-by and although it was closing time the friendly landlord allowed the party to take shelter. Nat thought it was great fun, especially as the pub was appropriately named the Bugle. Eventually, after it had rested for a while, with a spot of coax-ing Bob Panting managed to get the engine of the mini-bus back to life, so everyone piled on and happily arrived back in Gosport safely.

Other trips out of town for Gonella included several visits to

Cole Mathieson's Concorde Club at East Leigh near Southampton, Portsmouth Guildhall, and Fareham's Ferneham Hall to hear Chris Barber's band. Barber was delighted to receive Gonella in his dressing room but Barber's long-serving trumpeter Pat Halcox was even happier. Nat had been one of Halcox's idols for many years.

Other happy events brought Gonella back in touch with old friends. Ron Brown remembers seeing Nat on the occasion when bandleader Joe Loss brought his orchestra to the Portsmouth Guildhall. During the interval, Joe and Nat got so engrossed over chatting about old times that Joe almost missed his cue to go on-stage for the second half.

In 1987 more friends assembled for a special *Nat Gonella Tribute Show* held at the 100 Club, London's then 'home of traditional jazz' and Britain's longest-running club with (in 2005) a history of over sixty years. Many great names from the world of jazz were on hand to make the party go with a swing, including George Webb and his Dixielanders, Tommy Burton, Lonnie Donegan, George Chisholm, Alan Elsdon, Digby Fairweather, John Barnes, Ben Cohen, Dick Charlesworth, Maxine Daniels, Beryl Bryden, and Harry Gold and his Pieces of Eight. There were several happy reunions with names from Nat's past. Ted Easton flew in especially from Holland and sat behind the drums for an enthusiastic session. Pat Smuts, despite advancing years, sat in on sax for another long set, while Adelaide Hall delighted everyone by singing a couple of numbers.

The presence of former Georgians' bass player Charlie Winter was really the icing on the cake, for he and Nat had not met since that ill-fated tour of September 1939 when the group had to flee Sweden and Holland. Winter and Smuts bore no malice towards Nat after the unfortunate split.

Ron Brown made a personal note about the reunion between Nat and Charlie, who was living in Australia:

> In the summer of 1987, Charlie and his wife Rene came to Britain on holiday, staying with a friend at Weymouth in Dorset and I drove down to Weymouth to see them. Although by this time he was in his eighties and rather deaf, Charlie had an excellent memory and recounted many anecdotes from his Georgians days. The outcome of the meeting was that Charlie and Rene needed little persuasion to visit my wife and me in Gosport for a reunion with Nat. It was great to see Charlie and Nat relive those heady Georgians years of the 1930s, and more followed when I took our new friends to the Gosport Jazz Club to see Harry Gold and his Pieces of Eight, for it transpired that Charlie and Harry knew each other well from the old days. During their stay, Charlie and Rene were able to join us on the coach trip to the 100 Club show. They had a great time and as we said our farewells Charlie assured me that they would be saving up to come back again the following year. Sadly, it was not to be, for a few months later I received the news that Charlie Winter had passed away and his wife Rene followed him shortly afterwards.

Dorothy accompanied Nat to jazz nights locally, but her health had been declining steadily. At last it reached the stage where she was unable to climb the stairs of their cottage, forcing her to sleep in their small downstairs living room. Joyce Stone, visiting a friend near Gosport, learned something of the Gonella's problems and in 2004 she told Digby Fairweather the story. 'I said, "I'd love to go over to Gosport to meet one of Lew's musicians – a man called Nat Gonella." So my friend said, "I'll drive you over." We went there while he and Dorothy were still at the cottage; Nat had been ill in bed and had gone to the door to call for something. Dorothy had crawled up the stairs to bring it to him and when she opened the door it hit him hard and he was knocked out cold on the floor!'

Eventually, Nat and Dorothy moved to a warden-controlled flat in an elderly persons' complex, Raglan Court, conveniently situated fifty yards from where Gosport Jazz Club now held their weekly meetings. When taking a break from looking after his wife Gonella could often be found sitting on a seat outside his last home chatting to passers-by. Ron Brown recalls that Nat became friendly with several young mothers, for he loved children and he always made a fuss of Ron's five daughters whenever he went to the Browns' home. The seat became a form of meeting place where he entertained a new army of fans from dustmen to borough councillors. Even local taxi drivers remembered seeing him sitting on his bench.

Digby Fairweather visited Raglan Court on several occasions to see his friend, both casually and to interview him for Jazz FM in 1991 and later for Radio 2. 'The flat was charming and neat,' Fairweather recalled, 'with a wonderfully helpful nurse in attendance. Nat still had quite a lot of his souvenirs, including the handwritten solos he'd transcribed from Louis Armstrong records back in the 1920s, and a few pictures, which he was happy to show.' On one occasion, when he was still performing locally, Fairweather took him a mellophone – the one Gonella had left with Tiny Winters after he left Lew Stone:

> I thought he might like to start blowing again as mellophones are easy to play but I don't think he ever did. When I interviewed him we'd go into the lounge and it was plain that all the old people there – mainly ladies – adored him too.
>
> 'I've got some nice home-made jam for you, Nat.'
>
> 'Oh thank you, love.'
>
> 'I've nearly finished your sweater, Nat.'
>
> 'Oh that's lovely, love – thank you so much. Yes!'
>
> He was very gentle and Cockney-courteous. And when I inter-

viewed him the last time for Radio 2 I opened up with: 'Nat – it's a privilege,' and he said, 'Digby – I know!' Wonderful!

By now, though, Gonella's health was beginning to fail. 'A dodgy heart', as he termed it, may have caused his collapse outside a supermarket. 'I had a sort of fit,' he explained to Ron Brown with a chuckle, adding, 'You know, Ron, it took five men to hold me down!' Considering his height (five foot three inches) and weight (eight stone) this says something about his resilience and strength. The trumpeter was admitted to hospital on a number of occasions too; once, in October 1984, for a serious operation that left him very weak and his voice was almost non-existent. However, after an absence of over two months, Nat and Dorothy made an unheralded appearance at Pat and Tony Wing's New Year's Eve party at Gosport Jazz Club. As he entered the club, nearly two hundred merrymakers spontaneously applauded the couple as they made their way to the table. It was a most moving moment, for everybody that night was clearly so pleased to see him back. Later in the evening, the band struck up with 'When You're Smiling' and to everyone's delight Nat stood up without any prompting to jump on to the stage to take the microphone and provide the vocal. Although he was not quite back to his former lung power, he was clearly pleased and confided afterwards, 'Great! Quite honestly, after the sort of operation that I had, I thought that I would be singing more like Gracie Fields!'

There were other hospital visits too and, a couple of weeks after one such stay, Ron Brown was rushed into hospital and Nat went to visit him. By coincidence he was in the same bed that Nat had occupied, so it could be said that they were true bedfellows! Another time Gonella was admitted for a hip operation and Brown visited him on the ward a couple of days afterwards to find him in great form. The situation was hilarious, although the laughter was rather one-sided because Nat had taken out his false teeth to place them in a tissue on his bed-locker. Unknowingly, a nurse had come along and, thinking they were rubbish, disposed of them in the hospital incinerator. In these late years Nat's dentures – which he sometimes removed before singing – were a constant source of merriment at the jazz club. One lady fan even made a special velvet case for them with the legend 'Nashers!' tastefully embroidered across it.

Eventually, in 1994, the borough of Gosport recognised Nat officially and named a town square after their most famous resident. Adjacent to the town hall, Nat Gonella Square is a generous open space in which a showcase display tells his story while a sign hangs above. A large crowd gathered to see Humphrey Lyttelton host the unveiling ceremony and to hear Nat sing 'Georgia on My Mind' backed by a jazz band including Cuff Billett, Teddy Layton and bassist Alan Duddington. Thanking the Gosport officials for the gesture, the irrepressible Nat was quick to point out that the square was appropriately opposite Ladbroke's bookmakers. That morning he had had a phone call from trumpeter Kenny Baker offering congratulations too. 'Mind you,' said Baker, 'I've had a street in London named after me for fifty years!'

By now Dorothy Gonella's health was worsening. Digby Fairweather remembers seeing her, 'rolled up on the bed like a tiny – but still very pretty – ball. Nat could sometimes get very depressed at her decline, and once he rang me up very upset, opening his heart more than usual. I felt very sorry for him.'

Dorothy died on 4 March 1995, two days before Nat's eighty-seventh birthday concert. Arranged by Tony and Pat Wing, Nat's annual birthday parties at Gosport Jazz Club were a calendar highlight. The Club members doubted that he would attend this one, being so close to his sad loss. However, being the veteran trouper that he was, he made a brief appearance and it was a particularly poignant moment when he came on to the stage of the Thorngate Ballroom to take the microphone and sing 'I'm Confessing that I Love You'. This was the song he had always sung and dedicated to Dorothy at previous birthday concerts.

With Dorothy's passing, Gonella once more changed his way of living. He became more outgoing and – once again eager to perform – began guest appearances at jazz concerts and festivals countrywide. Among others these included yearly visits to the Isle of Man Jazz Festival and concert appearances, some of them in the company of Digby Fairweather. On 26 January 1996 he starred with the Great British Jazz Band, co-led by Pete Strange and Fairweather, at the Medina Theatre on the Isle of Wight. The concert was a sell-out three weeks in advance.

On 20 September the same year, Gonella returned to the Medina to guest with Digby Fairweather's Half-Dozen, a concert repeated at the same venue the following year, this time with Fairweather, the Unity Stompers, and the Goose Island Syncopators. Nat's friends John and Anna Wortham were always present at these and other less formal appearances. 'Nat was unfailingly cheerful and modest about the fact that he was remembered [and] that people still enjoyed his performances,' says Anna. 'At a charity concert at Alum Bay a torrential rainstorm flooded the stage, but he carried on, soaking wet, until it came close to all the musicians being electrocuted! Nothing fazed him – not even having to appear at the Queen Elizabeth Hall [in London in June 1996 with the Great British Jazz Band] in evening dress with ordinary trousers – his dress trousers had slipped off the hanger at the cleaners!' After the Alum Bay performance Nat walked up to the disabled people in the audience and spoke to each one.

Christmas concerts at the Purcell Room on London's South Bank (for John Woolf's Park Lane Group) followed in 1996 and 1997, in which Gonella guested with Fairweather's Half-Dozen. John and Anna Wortham drove him up to London and took great care of him. Gonella was a regular visitor to the Worthams' home on the Isle of Wight. 'I loved him,' says Anna. 'He retained a charming manner with women; one could see how attractive he must have been when young! He had always been a natty dresser and still wanted to look his best on-stage. So before a performance, I would brush his hair. We would sing "Blue Turning Grey Over You" and laugh together at the lines "I Run my Hands / Thru Silver Strands".'

Off-stage, Gonella was still a great gambler. 'His passion was the horses,' Anna remembers:

> He had to be taken into Ladbroke's to place his bets and then watched the results on TV. There never seemed to be any winnings to collect! He carried a dark-blue plastic bag at all times, containing an assortment of items: all his tablets, old betting slips, spare teeth and an electric razor. This went off on our way to a concert and until we traced the buzz we thought we had engine trouble! He talked about the old days: musicians and bandleaders, playing golf with Max Miller, enjoying football with George Formby, stories of Dorothy Squires, Gracie Fields, and Beryl Bryden, and his anecdotes were always amusing – never malicious.

Ron Brown thought at the time that, with Dorothy gone and his ninetieth birthday not far away, Nat had decided that he would go out with a bang. Although Ron had been trying for years to get Nat to attend a *Memory Lane* annual reunion for the magazine, Gonella surprised him by doing just that in 1997. Nat's friend John Pittard has memories of the day. 'I drove Nat up from Gosport to Joyce Stone's house… For me the most amazing part was listening to Nat talking to Joyce about her years as a debutante and the Stone years, more than sixty years before.' Joyce Stone also remembers this London visit. 'I put Nat and John up here at my home. I knew Nat always loved a cup of tea. So while he was getting ready for bed I made the tea and sat talking to John, and I said to call Nat, and along he comes in a pair of pyjamas. And I swear they had Mickey Mouse on the front or something of that sort.'

Nevertheless, Nat was beginning to show his age. Drummer Jim Byrne, who backed Gonella several times around the south coast, remembers that, 'At this time Nat almost had to be hauled up to sing. But once he was there the adrenalin took over and all of a sudden there he was at full speed.' The atmosphere of fun prevailed still.

In January 1997 came another extraordinary coincidence. At the age of eighty-eight Nat Gonella found himself once again at the top of Britain's pop charts. A trumpet passage from his recording of 'My Woman' with Lew Stone in 1932 had been sampled electronically by nouveau-pop band White Town into a hit record appropriately titled 'Your Woman'. The new version was computer-enhanced and slightly speeded up, but when it was played over the phone to Nat, the trumpeter was amazed. 'It's very flattering that people still listen to my old records,' he said. 'No money, of course,' he added with mild irritation.

A year later, on 8 February 1998, Gonella made his last recordings, produced by collector-authority Dave Bennett and subsequently issued on *Nat Gonella: A Jazz Legend Through the Years 1930–1998* by Avid Records. He sang nine titles accompanied by Kenny Baker (trumpet), Digby Fairweather (trumpet/cornet), Teddy Layton (clarinet/tenor), Martin

Litton (piano), Diz Disley (guitar) and Jack Fallon (bass). Fairweather remembers that 'by now Nat did look quite old. He sat by the piano for the session and sang his vocals straight down on to the tracks; no overdubbing. Everyone played well and Kenny Baker was marvellous, playing tremendously confidently as he always did with that huge sound and taking videofilm of the session when he wasn't playing. Nat looked across and at one point said, "You always were better than me!" rather ruefully. But he sang wonderfully.' The CD was completed with tracks recorded throughout Gonella's career, from Billy Cotton to the Georgia Jazz Band.

When Nat Gonella visited London for the last time in late February 1998, John Wortham accompanied him, ensuring that Nat took his medication on time and was as comfortable as possible. Nevertheless the trumpeter undertook a punishing schedule, including one day with two radio interviews and then a full show afterwards. Working every night with Fairweather's Half-Dozen at Knightsbridge's Pizza on the Park, he still sang with unerring swing, relaxed time and obvious enjoyment. Digby Fairweather remembers that:

> He was marvellous as usual, telling jokes, totally relaxed. And he was natural as can be – no airs and graces. He was billeted in a very basic hotel in Hounslow and there wasn't even a lounge. But when I offered to complain he said, 'Oh no! We don't mind. We can manage.' And he was just short of ninety. One of his favourite words was 'naturally'. And I think that's partly what endeared him to the audience – because he was so natural, not 'stagey' at all. And you know something else: his *time* was so perfect when he sang. But one strange thing happened. I knew that every night Nat would have to sing 'Georgia' but also knew that – originally – he sang it in D-flat, rather than F which most bands play it in. When they did, Nat used to alter the melody on the phrase 'just an old sweet song' which in F goes to a high E concert pitch. Nat

would sing down to a B instead, which is musically fine – but not the melody. So we played it in D-flat instead but Nat sang down anyhow – this time to a G concert!

On the last night I was quite worried. John Wortham and I had to help him up the stairs as he'd sung himself to a standstill amid the ovation. As we got him to the car and John and he drove away I wondered if I might not see him again. And I didn't – although I did try, very near the end. But it was a marvellous triumphant week for the old man!

On an earlier occasion Nat had told Fairweather why he was still pursuing life in the fast lane wherever he could. 'It's the excitement,' he explained. 'I still need it, you see.' Joyce Stone remembers a small illustration of the fact:

[My friend] Kirsteen and I drove over to Gosport after Dorothy had died but Nat of course was still at Raglan Court. And the girl who ran the home said, 'Oh, he's in hospital.' So in trepidation we drove to the Naval Hospital and when we got there and found the ward, his bed was empty and I immediately thought the worst. On the contrary, somebody else on the ward said, 'No, he's gone home.' So back we went to the home – and no, Nat had gone to this woman's house! So we went back next morning to see him and he still hadn't come home by eleven o'clock. Then he turned up in a taxi a bit the worse for wear, and was very surprised to see us. And he said to Kirsteen, 'Make us a cup of tea, love!' And she said, 'Nat, the milk's gone sour.' And he said, 'Doesn't matter. Just put it in with two spoons of sugar and I'll drink it anyway.' Which he did!

On Wednesday 4 March 1998 a capacity audience celebrated Nat Gonella's ninetieth birthday at Gosport Jazz Club. Kenny Baker, Beryl Bryden and Rosemary Squires were star guests, along with two bands: the Beachcombers and Brian White's Magna Jazz Band. When Nat arrived on-stage to sing his first song with trumpeter Baker, he received an ecstatic reception.

After his set a group of lady members ran to the stage to throw knickers at him, and Ron Brown will never forget the image of Nat finishing his set with a pair of red satin briefs round his head! Beryl Bryden, Nat's lifelong fan and one of Britain's most resilient female performers, was also in indomitable form, belting out favourites including 'Dr Jazz' and playing her silver-plated washboard with the same enthusiasm as fifty years before.

But time was running out for Nat. Early in August 1998 he had suffered an unfortunate fall and unknowingly broken his elbow. He was admitted to hospital for two operations to set, then reset, his elbow. 'Luckily,' says his daughter Natalie, 'I was able to visit Nat there; we shared lots of memories and managed a few laughs.' But then, after promising signs of recovery (a day before his death Gonella was sitting up in bed to read his get-well cards), he unexpectedly slipped into a coma. A cassette player was placed by his bedside playing jazz music, and visiting friends changed the tapes regularly. Then, on August 6, at ten in the evening, Britain's first star trumpeter, Nat Gonella, passed away; Natalie had been with her father until a few hours before he died.

His death was speedily acknowledged in the press. *The Times* and *Daily Telegraph* published detailed obituaries and south coast papers, including the *Portsmouth News* and *Southampton Echo*, devoted many pages both to his passing and the coming funeral. His Gosport friends were determined to give the trumpeter a suitably celebratory departure. The funeral took place at St Mary's Church, Alverstoke, on 20 August 1998. Over five hundred people packed into pews (including at least one of Nat's contemporaries from St Mary's, trombonist George Latimer, who by now was a Chelsea pensioner and dressed accordingly), while hundreds more listened outside on loudspeakers. A band led by Teddy Layton with Digby Fairweather on cornet played a selection of Gonella favourites and Fairweather delivered a warm and affectionate eulogy (subsequently published), 'which,' he later said, 'was the most important speech I'll ever make.' Singer Jo Baker rendered a poignant 'Georgia on My Mind', followed by a concluding 'Swing Low Sweet Chariot' accompanied by band and congregation. The entire event was captured on video.

The Excelsior Marching Band led the cortege to Ann's Hill Cemetery. With a top-hatted leader holding his brightly coloured umbrella, New Orleans-style, the procession moved slowly and with dignified restraint through the town along roads cordoned off by police. Then, on rounding the corner for the cemetery, the band raised the tempo and hundreds of marchers allowed themselves a smile. Amid the floral tributes laid by the grave was one from the Gosport Jazz Club, a bright golden-yellow wreath in the shape of a trumpet. Then, with the Excelsior band setting the pace, gaily decorated umbrellas were raised and hundreds of followers marched to a reception, for refreshments and a glorious jam session. Everyone was of the same opinion, felt Ron Brown: Nat would have loved it! Pianist/entertainer Tommy Burton – a regular visit to Gosport until his death in 2000 – said: 'Nat was a lovely person. I never heard anyone say anything bad about him.' And daughter Natalie concluded: 'moving to Gosport was the best thing that could have happened to Nat and Dorothy. I'm certain that the love and care he received in the town contributed to his longevity.'

On 10 March 1999, the first tribute evening for Nat Gonella was celebrated at Gosport Jazz Club with Rosemary Squires, Digby Fairweather and Laurie Chescoe's Goodtime Jazz Band.

Adjacent to Gonella's old seat outside Raglan Court, a memorial was erected: a wrought-iron trumpet, five feet high, with moveable valves and music notation attached, depicting the opening notes of 'Georgia on My Mind'. The location of this ambitious monument was no accident; Gonella had sometimes light-heartedly complained of 'draughts' as he sat on the street. Then, some months after his funeral, when their grave had settled, a stone was set at its head marked with the names of Nat and Dorothy Gonella and engraved with an image of a gold trumpet.

Since then, the Nat Gonella Fund has been established by Natalie Wilson with Pat and Tony Wing for the benefit of children of poor families in Gosport, through monies raised from raffles at the jazz club and other local events. After putting her father's trumpet to auction, Natalie donated the proceeds to the fund. As a result, scores of local children have been bought clothing (principally new shoes), given Christmas parties and taken for countryside outings and to leisure parks in Hampshire. The cause would have delighted Nat Gonella, whose memories included barefoot children playing in the London streets around Kings Cross.

Bruts Gonella had worked with Sid Millward and Harry Gold in 1952–54 and moved to Australia in 1964. He continued playing with big bands and small groups in New South Wales until a serious illness in the 1980s ended his playing career. He died in 2002, one year after the death of his wife, Shelley. 'He just gave up, really, after that,' says Natalie Wilson, 'just stayed on his own and faded away.' It's interesting to note that all three of the Gonella family who attended St Mary's Guardian School achieved the age of ninety and died one after the other at two-year intervals.

Nevertheless the name of Britain's first star jazz trumpeter lives on securely in jazz history. In an interview for the *Sunday Express*, 4 March 1962, when the 'trad boom' had brought him back to national prominence, Nat Gonella said, 'If I should die tomorrow I wouldn't regret a single thing. I've had a million laughs.' Another thirty-six years were in store for him; years in which Nat's name first receded, then gradually found its way back into the national spotlight, exactly as he deserved.

Gonella's *Modern Style Trumpet Playing* states: 'Try to make the music into words and "speak" them on your instrument as you would in conversation, with a pause here, an inflection there, an accentuation here – and so on. To sum up – put some "feeling" into it.' That is what Nat Gonella did with his life. And jazz music was the richer for it.

Afterword*

by Digby Fairweather

Perhaps, as Whitney Balliett once wrote, nostalgia is cheap witchcraft. But Nat Gonella and his Georgians will always be linked with an early memory for me: of sitting on the deep green inlaid arm of my father's comfortable armchair, glancing through sunshot windows to waving green fields, and scanning his old EMI catalogues for jazz entries. The feeling was exciting and one degree furtive – akin to thumbing through his *Lilliput* magazines in search of their one haughty pin-up. The EMI catalogue was equally sparing with its jazz délices, but one name appeared with reliable frequency – Nat Gonella.

The name on its own was jazzy enough. A lucky combination of happy accidents (Christian name Nathaniel, surname an Italian inheritance) — somehow ensured that he was already a great jazzman. 'The Georgians' sounded exactly right too, and so did the tunes they played: jazz standards, swing songs of the day, and intriguing novelties that cross-fertilized the jazz aesthetic with an injection of music hall, well within the sounds of Bow Bells and Billy Cotton. It was a heady brew, but hard to track down; no records in the cupboard or at the local shop. So Bing Crosby and Louis Armstrong continued their carillon uninterrupted, the name of Nat Gonella, for now, an intriguing echo in the breeze.

*Adapted from the foreword to the first edition, 1985.

For a schoolboy long on enthusiasm but short on pocket money, the best way to buy records was from the local junkshop, run by Harry Strauss, a patient saint of a man. Day after day, Harry put up with my determined re-searching of the same pile of old 78s. I found lots of Harry James and Artie Shaw, plenty of Sid Phillips, Humphrey Lyttelton and Freddy Randall, and occasionally a Joe Daniels or a Louis Armstrong, but never a Nat Gonella.

Many years passed before I found an original Gonella record. There it was, at the bottom of a pile of once-loved old records in an antique shop. It was a maroon-labelled, gold-lettered revelation that proclaimed: 'Don't Cross Your Fingers, Cross Your Heart', sung and played by Nat, backed with 'Stop Beating Around the Mulberry Bush'. I hurried home to make my first discoveries.

The loudspeaker revealed a warm rhythmic singer bouncing through a boldly-intervalled swing tune of the type that became the Second World War's first casualty. A trumpet of gold tone, assured command and able swing, through which an English promise ran, as old and bold as John Bull himself. A picture of Nat Gonella, jazz trumpeter, began to emerge. More detail was added when an old friend and Gonella fan presented me with a cassette of vintage Georgians. I quickly observed that the celebrated Gonella-Armstrong resemblance was much over-played. The Georgia boy's warm, intense, highly-correct trumpet playing, with its curt tonguing and studious vibrato, rang a bell for Kneller Hall – twenty miles west of his Islington home — as well as New Orleans. The result was a compelling swing trumpeter, without the simple perfection that made Armstrong a genius but with a facility and direct lyricism that found an echo in players such as Mouse Randolph and Wingy Manone. Gonella sounded like such men, but historically he was their peer, and greater than most. It may have been that Louis would have run him off the stage had they met in some fantasy-world cutting contest, but fine second liners like Mouse, Wingy or Herman Autry would have been out in the street before Nat.

So, where, if anywhere, were the similarities with Louis? Certainly they existed, in some of the technical facility to begin with. Nat could as easily lead the Roy Fox brass section as he could play creative jazz. He had the confidence of a natural leader: confidence enough to transfer his in-flight imagination unflawed to records, and on occasion to play for Louis himself. He had the strength of character, akin to Louis, to let his trumpet-playing survive all the rigours and pressures of show-business and stardom. And, like Louis, he also had the physical and mental strength and discipline to play to the top of his range every night, without allowing his art to be dulled by beautiful girls, late nights, or wondering whether he would make the top E at the close of 'Basin Street Blues'.

To experience his pure joy of playing, listen to the 1934 recording that he made with Brian Lawrance: 'Sweet Sue, Just You'. There's that broad-as-a-mile British sound, and the confident inspiration that slowly and naturally brings the performance to a climax, plus the effortless movement between registers, copybook accuracy and facility in top registers. Above all, the technical *joie de vivre*, that transmits itself to a performance when a trumpet player knows that he is playing well, is much in evidence. If a distinction has to be made, for Louis Armstrong the *joie de vivre* made itself apparent in the top one hundred elemental top Cs of 'Shine'. For Nat Gonella, it was the cheeky 'watch-me-now' triple-tongued runs of 'Sweet Sue, Just You' that anticipated Charlie Shavers by a good five years, and were created by Nat from a jazz vacuum. One thing is clear, Armstrong and Gonella together were young men exulting in their command over that physically challenging – and rewarding – adversary, the trumpet. And jazz was all the richer for it.

Progressing through the dance music and jazz scene of the 1930s, Nat's style broadened with the music trends of the war years. Listen to the New Georgians in 'Song of Songs'. Without losing its identity, the trumpet sound has moved with the times. An on-form Harry James might have played little better than Gonella on this record. It was only with the advent of bebop that our subject, for once, stopped short. His reaction to the highly self-conscious innovation of bop was simple, and after a short flirtation, final. 'Gas oven music' he called it, and agree or not, his three-word analysis carried the same conviction as Louis Armstrong's statement, 'Man you don't pose, never.' While bebop was never truly a pose, for Britain's first classic jazz trumpeter – then approaching forty — it really had to be.

Over the following years, Nat's fortunes fluctuated considerably: a return to the music hall, playing in small clubs and pubs, and on occasion, nowhere. Where he had once earned thousands, he was glad to take home a few pounds in order to survive. But, as always, there was that friendly Cockney voice that tried to persuade you that, 'it was really all a bit of a lark,' nothing more. 'Just a bit of a lark' is the way that Nat Gonella would have you remember his life but, for me, his story – supreme success though it is – is also a grand example of fate at her most ungenerous. At least three luckless 'invasions' – Poland in 1939, modern jazz in 1946, and Merseybeat in 1962 – dealt hammer blows to a career that should have achieved immortality by the time he was fifty.

But his life — up, down, and all ways – impinged on our lives too. The vision you carry with you depends on when, for you, it happened first. It could have been when Nat emerged from behind some Moss Empire curtain in the thirties to climb an effortless top C. It could have been when, smiling and philosophical, he returned to the jazz scene with an all-star band in the early 1960s. Or maybe your vision is of the youthful, impish man on the stage of Gosport Jazz Club in the 1980s mugging his way through 'St James Infirmary' for a delighted crowd. My own vision is a composite, drawn from a picture painted in words by friend Tiny Winters. In this vision a young swing trumpeter in a check jacket walks jauntily out of a smoky Bag o' Nails Club into the morning air of a Mayfair dawn. His trumpet is under his arm, and all the world is at his feet.

Ladies and Gentlemen: we present the last king, the first legend of British jazz... Nat Gonella and his story. Ring up the happy curtain.

Digby Fairweather

Nat Gonella on CD and LP

A partial listing of albums issued under Nat Gonella's name or featuring him. All recorded in London unless otherwise stated. For a full discography to 1987 see Ron Brown, *The Gonella Discography* (Gosport, 1987).

CDs

Igor Bourco's Uralsky Jazzmen, featuring Nat Gonella and Beryl Bryden, *Oh! Mo'nah.* Jazz Between the Dykes JBTD 9721. Recorded in the Netherlands, 1997.

Nat Gonella, *A Jazz Legend Through the Years 1930-1998.* Avid AMSC 634. Compilation (1998) of recordings spanning Gonella's entire career.

Nat Gonella, *The Young Nat Gonella.* Retrieval RTR 79022. Compilation (1999) of recordings from 1930-1936.

Nat Gonella, *Georgia on my Mind.* ASV AJA 5300. Compilation (1998) of recordings from 1931-1941.

Nat Gonella and his Georgians, *Pennies from Heaven.* Soundwaves SWN CD 014. Compilation (1997) of recordings from 1935-1938.

Nat Gonella, *I Can't Dance.* Object Jazz Collection ORO 106. Compilation (1990) of recordings from 1935-1939.

Nat Gonella, *The Legendary Big Bands.* Pulse PLS CD 427. Compilation (2000) of recordings from 1935-1939.

Nat Gonella, *Nat Gonella and his Georgians.* Flapper PAST CD 9750. Compilation (c.1990) of recordings from 1935-1940.

Nat Gonella, *The Nat Gonella Collection.* HMV Easy 5340032. Compilation (2001) of recordings from 1935-1941.

Nat Gonella, *Blow That Horn.* Sun 2144. Compilation (2003) of recordings from 1935-1941.

Nat Gonella and his Georgians, *You Must Have Been a Beautiful Baby*. Memory Lane PGN CD 853. Compilation (2001) of recordings from 1935-1946.

Nat Gonella, *Nat and the Boys: jazz and dance music of the 1930s played and sung by `the British Louis Armstrong' Nat Gonella*. President PAR2007. CD reissue of *Nat Gonella Scrapbook* LP (listed below).

Nat Gonella and his New Georgians, *Naturally Gonella*. Empress RAJCD 804. Compilation (1993) of recordings from 1940-1941.

Nat Gonella, *The Dance Band Years*. Pulse PDS CD 552 (double CD). Compilation (1997) of New Georgians Big Band recordings from 1940-1946.

Lew Stone, *A Tribute to Lew Stone: The Legendary Monseigneur Band*. Claves CD 50-9507/9 (box set of three CDs). Compilation (2003) of recordings from 1932-1934.

White Town, *Abort, Retry, Fail / Your Woman*. Chrysalis 7243 83629 2 4 (CD single). `Your Woman', recorded 1997, features Gonella on sampled trumpet.

LPs

Johnny Claes and Nat Gonella, *The Swinging 40s*. Reflections C5-544. Compilation (1989) of New Georgians recordings from 1940-1941.

Billy Cotton and his Band featuring Nat Gonella, *That Rhythm Man*. Saville Records SVL 149. Compilation (1982) of recordings from 1928-1931.

Roy Fox and his Band, *Hello Ladies and Gentlemen, This is Roy Fox Speaking*. Ace of Clubs (Decca) Treasury Series ACL 1172. Compilation of 1931-1932 recordings from the Monseigneur Restaurant, Piccadilly.

Nat Gonella, *Nat Gonella and his Trumpet*. Ace of Clubs (Decca) Treasury Series ACL 1241. Compilation (1967) of recordings from 1932-1934.

Nat Gonella, *Georgia on my Mind*. Decca Recollections Series RFL 12. Compilation (1981) of recordings from 1932-1946.

Nat Gonella and his Georgians, *Mr. Rhythm Man*. EMI EG 26 0 1881-4. Compilation (1984) of recordings from 1934-5.

Nat Gonella and his Georgians, *Crazy Valves*. ASV Living Era AJA 5055. Compilation (1988) of recordings from 1934-7.

Nat Gonella and his Georgians, *Naturally Gonella*. Conifer CHD 129. Compilation (1986) of recordings from 1935.

Nat Gonella, *Yeah man!* Harlequin HQ3019. Compilation (1988) of recordings from 1935-1937.

Nat Gonella and his Georgians, *Mister Rhythm Man*. Historia Top Classic H639. German compilation (1970) of recordings from 1935-1939.

Nat Gonella and his Georgians, *The Georgia Boy from London*. EMI PMC 7149. Compilation (1972) of recordings from 1935-1941. Reissued (1980) as EMI Retrospect Series SH369.

Nat Gonella, *The Golden Age of Nat Gonella and his Georgians*. EMI GX 4125361. Compilation (1985) of recordings from 1935-1941.

Nat Gonella and his Georgians, *Georgia on my Mind*. World Records SH369. Compilation (1980) of recordings from 1935-1942.

Nat Gonella and his Georgians, *How'm I Doin'?* Old Bean OLD 11. Compilation (1987) of recordings from 1936.

Nat Gonella and his Georgians, *The Nat Gonella Scrapbook*. Joy Records D284. Compilation (1985) of radio and live recordings from the 1930s.

Nat Gonella's Georgia Jazzband, *Jazz at the Cottage*. 77 Records 77LP/20. Recorded 1958.

Nat Gonella and his Strong Arm Men, *Salute to Satchmo*. Columbia 33S 1146. Recorded 1959.

Nat Gonella's Georgia Jazz Band, *Runnin' Wild*. 77 Records 77LEU 12/48. Issue (1973) of club and studio recordings from 1960 plus reissue of some tracks from 77LP/20. Reissued (1985) with three additional tracks as Harlequin HQ 3003.

Nat Gonella and his Band, *The Nat Gonella Story*. Philips 6459 218. Recorded February 1961.

Nat Gonella and others, Lionel Bart's *Oliver*. ARC Society SOC 1002 / Presto PRE 649. Recorded 1965.

Nat Gonella and Beryl Bryden with Ted Easton's Jazz Band, *When You're Smiling*. CNR Records CNR 385 226. Recorded in Scheveningen, Holland, January 1970.

Nat Gonella, *The Music Goes 'Round and 'Round*. CNR Records CNR 540 023. Recorded in Scheveningen, Holland, May 1975.

Nat Gonella with Ted Easton's Band, *My Favourite Things*. Riff 659016. Recorded in Scheveningen, Holland, May 1975.

Nat Gonella with Ted Easton's Band, *Wishing You a Swinging Christmas*. CNR Records CNR 657 525. Recorded in Holland, October 1975.

Harry Roy and his Famous Band / Nat Gonella and his Georgians, *Bands on Film*. World Records SH 197. Soundtrack issued 1976, of 1935 band short.

Index

Also by Digby Fairweather

Notes from a Jazz Life

'Entertaining and well-written... reflects the generous-spirited and enthusiastic character of an exceptionally gifted trumpeter,' *Jazz Journal*.

'Thoroughly entertaining and yet thoughtful... a fascinating look at the last 30 odd years of a big slice of the British jazz scene,' *Musician*.

'A fund of diverting jazz stories told with disarming modesty and humour,' *Jazz Rag*.

Illustrations by Peter Manders and Humphrey Lyttelton.

£7.99

Other jazz books from Northway

Jim Godbolt

A History of Jazz in Britain
1919-50

Revised edition

hardback

£16.99

Harry Gold

Gold, Doubloons and
Pieces of Eight

paperback

£10.99